Word Myths

Word Myths

/'wərd ˌmiTHs/

Debunking Linguistic
Urban Legends

David Wilton

Illustrated by
Ivan Brunetti

OXFORD
UNIVERSITY PRESS

2009

OXFORD
UNIVERSITY PRESS

Oxford New York
Auckland Bangkok Buenos Aires Cape Town Chennai
Dar es Salaam Delhi Hong Kong Istanbul Karachi Kolkata
Kuala Lumpur Madrid Melbourne Mexico City Mumbai Nairobi
São Paulo Shanghai Taipei Tokyo Toronto

Published by Oxford University Press, Inc.
198 Madison Avenue, New York, New York 10016

www.oup.com

Library of Congress Cataloging-in-Publication Data
Wilton, David, 1963–
Word myths : debunking linguistic urban legends /
by David Wilton.
p. cm. — Includes bibliographical references and index.
ISBN 978-0-19-537557-2
1. English language—Etymology.
2. Language and languages—Folklore.
I. Title.
PE1584.W55 2004   422—dc22   2004005598

All artwork used with the permission of the artist, Ivan Brunetti © 2004.
www.ivanbrunetti.com

Printed in the United States of America
on acid-free paper

Contents /ˈkänˌtents/

Acknowledgments /akˈnälijmənts/

N umerous people assisted in the preparation of this book. First among them is Erin McKean, my editor at Oxford University Press. Erin guided me through multiple versions of the book proposal and was the source of some great ideas and much inspiration.

Some of the etymological debunkings and datings contained herein are based on data collected by Barry Popik and Gerald Cohen. Barry also answered some particular questions of mine, for which I am most grateful. Allan Metcalf, David Barnhart, and Jesse Sheidlower provided background information about work they had previously published. ADS member Carol Braham and Martha Gilland, a member of Senator Zell Miller's staff, both provided citations for hard-to-find books. David and Barbara Mikkelson, editors of the *Urban Legends Reference Pages* at www.snopes.com, provided the jumping-off point for my research into some of the legends presented here. Their excellent website pointed me toward some invaluable sources of information and saved me countless hours of research.

I owe a special debt of gratitude to my cousin Judith Bennett of the University of North Carolina for putting me in initial contact with the editors at Oxford and short-circuiting the process of sending out blind queries and proposals. Other family members who gave direct assistance were Shirley and Jim Wilton, my mother and brother, respectively, who helped proofread and edit the proposal and manuscript. (Any errors, of course, are mine and not theirs.) My other brother, Carlos, provided background material on the *icthys* acronym.

Finally, I would like to give a shout out to the gang who regularly contributes to my website's online discussion forum. They have made the last few years of running my website a joy. I will not attempt to list them all for fear of leaving someone out, but I have to mention Barry Gehm, a.k.a. "Dr. Techie," who coined the acronym CANOE, or Conspiracy to Attribute Nautical Origins to Everything, a term that I have shamelessly appropriated as a chapter title.

Word Myths

Introduction

All of us are familiar with urban legends. Even if you are not familiar with the term *urban legend*, it is a near certainty that you have heard, or even told, one. One infamous urban legend is "The Hook," about an escapee from a lunatic asylum, who has a hook for a hand and leaves it in the door handle of a car parked in lover's lane. Then there is the one about the teenage babysitter, high on LSD, who puts the baby in the oven thinking it is a turkey. Others are not so gruesome. There is "Sit, Lady," in which two middle-aged, white women are in an elevator in Las Vegas (or Atlantic City or New York City or . . .), when a large, African-American man, leading a fierce-looking dog by a leash, enters the elevator and says, "Sit, Lady!" The two women dutifully comply only to see the man breaking out in laughter since "Lady" is the name of his dog.

In the story, the man is famous (usually baseball player Reggie Jackson, but sometimes singer Lionel Richie or comedian Eddie Murphy), and the story ends with the amused celebrity sending the women flowers and treating them to dinner and a night out on the town.

These are classic urban legends. The term *urban folklore* (or *myth* or *legend*) dates to 1960, and these legends are so called because they are stories of industrial societies.[1] Urban legends do not get their name because they necessarily refer to events that supposedly happened in cities. Rather, they are called that because they are tales, usually cautionary, told by people who live in our modern, urbanized society. There is, however, another type of folklore that is very much like these classic urban legends. These are what I call *linguistic urban legends*. Rather than propagating cautionary tales about the dangers of modern life, linguistic urban legends propagate stories and "facts" about language and words.

You have probably heard these linguistic legends too. Did you ever think that *Ring around the Rosie* made reference to the Black Death of the Middle Ages? Or that *the whole nine yards* refers to the length of a machine-gun ammo belt on a World War II fighter plane? Or perhaps that Eskimos have 500 words for snow? If so, then you have been taken in by a linguistic urban legend.

What Is a Linguistic Urban Legend?

Linguistic urban legends do not quite fit the classic definition of an urban legend, but they are very similar. The Usenet newsgroup alt.folklore.urban defines the term *urban legend* as follows:

An urban legend:
- Appears mysteriously and spreads spontaneously in varying forms.
- Contains elements of humor or horror (the horror often "punishes" someone who flouts society's conventions).
- Makes good storytelling.
- Does *not* have to be false, although most are. [Urban legends] often have a basis in fact, but it is their life after-the-fact (particularly in reference to the second and third points) that gives them particular interest.[2]

It is the second point in the definition that tends to pose problems for linguistic urban legends. Linguistic urban legends do arise mysteriously and spread widely. As we shall see, many of them mutate into different versions of the same basic truth. Some make good storytelling, others are only an interesting bit of trivia. While most are false, almost all linguistic urban legends have some grain of truth at the core that is grossly distorted in their retelling.

But unlike traditional urban legends, linguistic urban legends usually do not contain elements of horror or humor. As a rule, they do not depict punishment of those that flout convention. Most of them do, however, contain a core element that makes them popular, that makes us want to keep telling them. With this slight variation, linguistic urban legends are like their classic cousins.

Where Do They Come From?

Tracing the origins of urban legends, traditional or linguistic, is usually a futile task. The alt.folklore.urban definition says they "appear mysteriously" and it is rare to trace a legend back to a definite point of origin. While finding a specific origin is usually impossible, we can often bind the origin of a legend in time. We know, for example, that the legend of the sports-writing term *upset,* coming from a 1919 horse race, in which a horse of that name beat the famed Man o' War (chapter 5, p. 148) must have arisen sometime during or after that year. We often can trace a legend back to a particular telling of it, but that does not mean the legend is not older. For example, we know that the phrase *mind your Ps and Qs* (see chapter 4, p. 108) comes from chalkboard tallies of bar tabs and dates to at least 1852 because a magazine article from that year describes the legend. But when and where did it arise? All we know is that it was sometime before 1852.

Sometimes we can date specific details of the story, but not the story itself. The "Pluck Yew" story (chapter 3, p. 89) is a good example. On April 6, 1996, the National Public Radio show *Car Talk* featured a "Puzzler" about English archers at the Battle of Agincourt. Subsequently, the "Pluck Yew" story appears on the internet, crediting that show as the source. Now the detail about *Car Talk* is certainly from the spring of 1996, but the story about archers at Agincourt is undoubtedly older.

So, is the best we can do is say they "appear mysteriously"? That is not very satisfying and we can often do better. Many of these tales arise from three particular circumstances: jokes, speculation, and distorted facts.

Many of the legends described here began life as jokes. The aforementioned "Pluck Yew" story is a good example. Whoever first came up with the explanation was almost certainly joking. It is clever word play, not a serious etymology. Those who tell the story may or may not believe it, but somewhere along the line some people started taking the story seriously. Another example is the story that John F. Kennedy's famous "Ich bin en Berliner" line actually means, "I am a jelly doughnut" (chapter 7, p. 186). This tale evidently began life in the routines of one or more German stand-up comedians. One subcategory of joke is the hoax. Some tales began this way, with the "Life in the 1500s" (chapter 2, p. 61) e-mail hoax being a prime example.

Other linguistic urban legends begin as speculation or hypotheses. For example, one wonders about the origins of the phrase *let the cat out of the bag* (chapter 4, p. 104). One speculates that it refers to the whip, or cat o' nine tails, used on ships to punish sailors. The cat, as it was called, was usually kept in a bag to protect it from the salt air. The hypothesis suggests that the phrase refers to a criminal act that causes the ship's officers to remove the whip from its bag to punish the guilty. This is simply speculation with no evidence to support it, but as this speculation is passed from one person to another, it loses its tentative nature and becomes a "fact."

The third path, distorted facts, is rarer—a story with a kernel of truth that is changed or distorted in the telling, much like the childhood game of "telephone" or "whispers." A good example is the legend that Eskimos have 500 words for snow (chapter 1, p. 50). In the early twentieth century, it was observed that Eskimos could create a large number of "words" from a handful of roots to describe different types of snow. As the story was passed from person to person, pertinent details were lost and the significance of the story reversed itself. Instead of being about a few basic roots, it became about the large number of products those roots generated.

How Do They Vary?

Most of these linguistic legends vary in the telling, distorting the basic facts in some way or another. The most common way is for the details regarding the particular circumstances to change. Perhaps the best example is *the whole nine yards* (chapter 1, p. 34). Often the tale is told that the phrase refers to nine yards of fabric. It is how the nine yards of cloth are used that changes with the telling. Sometimes it is a kilt, other times a man's suit or a burial shroud. Sometimes, it is supposed to be the standard length of a bolt of cloth with the caution that shopkeepers often short the customer and give less than the full length. Which version is told depends on the point the teller wishes to make. If one is proud of one's Scottish ancestry, the kilt story is told. If one wishes to give an example of duplicitous shopkeepers, it is a bolt of cloth, not a kilt.

The other main pattern of variation is lexicographic. The story remains the same but the relevant word changes with the telling. A prime example of this is the number of stories about prisoners wearing clothing emblazoned with an acronym of their crime. Sometimes this is *fuck*, standing for *For Unlawful Carnal Knowledge* (chapter 3, p. 87). Other times the word is *wogs*, standing for *Working on Government Service* (chapter 3, p. 95). One story has prisoners in the U.S. Civil War wearing *AWOL* on their clothes (chapter 3, p. 84). In this last case, *AWOL* is indeed an acronym, for Away With Out Leave, but the acronym does not date to the Civil War and prisoners did not wear it on their clothes.

Often though, the pattern is not that specific. We see a large number of false acronymic origins. Similarly, there are false eponyms, words from people's names, or words ascribed nautical origins that are not supported by evidence. The details in each story are quite different, but the basic pattern of how a word is said to have come into being is the same.

Why Do We Tell Them?

While some linguistic urban legends do contain elements of humor or horror, most do not. They hardly ever punish those who flout convention. They are usually not cautionary. Yet, they are similar to traditional urban legends in that the story-teller believes the tale has a valuable message. For instance, that we want to associate a child's nursery rhyme with some tribal memory of the Black Death tells us something about ourselves. This message has a "truth," even if the facts are false. Even if they are factually incorrect, they contain an element of truth— or more accurately, the truth, as we would like it to be.

If these legends were simply errors, nothing more than incorrect facts, they would not persist. They would be easily corrected and the legends would die. They would not disappear all at once, of course. It would take some time for the correct facts to spread, but inevitably and in reasonably short order the correct facts would assert themselves. But they do not do so. The legends persist, defying correction.

Take the origin of *Windy City*, for example (chapter 1, p. 54). The correct origin of this nickname for Chicago has been established and readily available for over fifty years. Anyone doing even the most cursory research cannot help but stumble across the true story. Yet almost without exception, every time a newspaper article brings up the subject they print the false legend instead of the truth. Is this because journalists are incompetents who do not know enough to crack open a dictionary when a question about word origins arises? No. As a group, journalists are intelligent and capable people who have an innate desire to get at the truth. Then why do they keep printing the false story? They do so because the appeal of the legend overwhelms the appeal of printing the truth.

The legend of the origin of *Windy City* is about the rivalry of two great cities. It is about the wild and woolly West challenging the staid establishment of the East. It is about politics and politicians. And it is about journalism. (And journalists love to write about themselves and their profession.) Compared to this, the winds off of Lake Michigan are just plain boring. It is a good story; why mess it up with the truth?

As we examine the different linguistic urban legends presented here, several reasons for their appeal keep recurring. Not all of these reasons are present in each legend, of course, but at least one appears in most:

- They are just plain fun. Some of these legends make good storytelling. We are social creatures and we simply cannot resist the appeal of a good tale.
- They strengthen and validate group identity. These groups can be ethnic, national, professional, or of another type. The myth that America is named after Richard Ameryk, a fifteenth-century Bristol merchant, is rooted in Welsh and English national pride (chapter 4, p. 123). Or if you are from the Appalachia, a claim that you speak the language of Shakespeare is an antidote to social and economic disadvantages that your accent brings (chapter 1, p. 44).
- Linguistic legends can also validate group identity in negative ways, by reinforcing racist and xenophobic ideas. These can be relatively neutral, as in the idea that Eskimos are strange and different because they have 500 words for snow (chapter 1, p. 50). Or they can be more hurtful.

- A legend may appeal to an individual's interests. Those who have an interest in the sea and things nautical, for example, tend to ascribe nautical origins to words. Those fascinated by railroads tend to associate phrases like *balling the jack* and *balls to the wall* with trains (chapter 4, p. 113). Civil War buffs spread the legend that General Hooker is an eponym for the word *hooker*, a prostitute (chapter 5, p. 130), and that the acronym *AWOL* was used in the 1860s (chapter 3, p. 84).
- Legends can serve a political purpose. The idea that *picnic* is associated with the lynching of Blacks in the American South conveys an element of personal horror that detached and factual historical accounts of the abuses suffered by African Americans often lack (chapter 6, p. 157).
- One specialized political purpose is to lampoon the high and mighty. From implying that William the Conqueror's mother was the original *harlot* (chapter 5, p. 131) to Andrew Jackson's bad spelling resulting in the word *OK* (chapter 1, p. 28), linguistic urban legends often take aim at rulers, politicians, or big corporations. Anyone or anything that is rich and powerful is vulnerable.
- Economic purposes can also be served by these stories, which are often told in the context of marketing campaigns. One can hardly read an advertisement for a book on international marketing or for business translation services without running into *bite the wax tadpole* or the Chevy Nova legend (chapter 7, p. 188).
- Euphemism is a driving force behind some of these legends. People tell stories about how it should be *tinker's dam*, not *tinker's damn* (chapter 6, p. 182) and how *cold enough to freeze the balls off a brass monkey.* (chapter 4, p. 106) refers to racks of cannonballs instead of simian anatomy in order to make the phrases more palatable for polite society.

- Other legends are told because they are examples of word play and humor. Notable among these are all the stories that attribute acronymic origins to words. People love word play and games and this is reflected in many of the legends. Also, some of the legends, such as the infamous *ship high in transit* story (chapter 3, p. 79), are originally intended as jokes, but are believed to be true by some.
- Finally, one of the most compelling reasons for telling these tales is that they explain mysteries. That they give false or undocumented explanations is beside the point. To say something is unknown is profoundly unsatisfying. So, if an explanation is not available, we will create one.

How Are They Told?

There is a distinct difference in how linguistic urban legends are told or transmitted as opposed to traditional urban legends. For traditional legends—like *The Hook* or *Sit Lady!*—the primary means of transmission is oral. We tell these stories to one another in casual conversation. They rarely appear in published sources, other than in books about urban legends.

Traditional urban legends are usually stories. They have plot arcs and often end with an element of horror or humor. Because of this, they lend themselves very well to oral transmission. Linguistic urban legends are less apt to be told orally. As stand alones, they seldom are complete stories. This does not mean that they are not told in casual conversation. They most certainly are. They are just not as compelling in the oral medium, in and of themselves, as their traditional cousins.

Traditional urban legends are also usually about specific events and as a result are less likely to appear in published sources. The classic urban legends, if true, could be nailed down by questions like who, what, when, and where. The place where event-driven stories are traditionally told is in newspapers and other news media. Reporters are very good about asking the questions who, what, when, and where and are also good about verifying those specific facts. As a result, reporters are pretty good at ferreting out the lack of truth behind traditional urban legends and such tales seldom make it into published media. Reporters make mistakes of course, but as a general rule classic urban legends do not make it into print. And if they do, it is usually as a general warning, not as a specific factual event. For example, every October numerous newspaper stories warn of the potential for poison in Halloween candy, but none are about specific cases—because it rarely, if ever, happens.

Other published media, books, documentaries, and the like, usually rely on news media, especially newspapers, for facts about events. If events are not reported by newspapers, they generally do not make it into other published sources.

This is not the case with tales that are not about events, like most linguistic urban legends. The questions who, what, when, and where are rarely applicable to linguistic urban legends. We can, for instance, verify that Joseph Hooker commanded the Army of the Potomac for a brief period during the Civil War. He was known for his loose moral character and tolerance of various debaucheries among his officers and men. But asking the "W questions" and verifying the answers will not tell us whether or not the word *hooker* comes from his name.

Instead of asking the W questions for such stories, we usually rely on experts, such as historians, to verify the fact. The trouble is what makes a person an expert in one field does make her one in linguistics or etymology. Complicating this, linguistic urban legends are rarely told as the main point of a narrative. Instead, they are usually used to illustrate a minor point or simply to provide an entertaining digression. Writers, even serious and dedicated scholars, are less likely to verify such digressions than they are the central points of their arguments. For example, in the second volume of his famous history of the Civil War, historian Shelby Foote tells us that General Hooker gave us the word *hooker* meaning a prostitute.[3] Foote is a superb and well-respected historian. But while we can rely on him to accurately give us the position of Armistead's brigade during Pickett's Charge, he probably did not even attempt to verify the etymological *hooker* tidbit. Another example is in Ken Burns's multipart documentary *Jazz*. In it, trumpeter Wynton Marsalis tells us the origin of the word *jazz* (see chapter 4, p. 116). He, not unexpectedly to those of us that study these things, gets it wrong. Marsalis may be the greatest trumpet player of our time, but he is a questionable authority on etymology.

Why not trust people like Foote or Marsalis on questions about words relating to their fields? After all, they are masters of their particular crafts. The reason is that their crafts are not linguistics and etymology. Foote will examine official documents, maps, letters, and diaries to find out what happened in a particular battle, but he is not likely to start looking in dictionaries from the 1840s to look for early appearances of the word *hooker*. Marsalis's knowledge of the origin of *jazz* is undoubtedly from conversations with fellow musicians. Oral traditions like this are sometimes correct or at least can provide clues as to where to look. Listening to him may be a good place to start a search for the origin of *jazz*, but it is not the place to finish.

The appearance of these linguistic legends in published sources gives them credence. Now even people who might normally exhibit a fair degree of skepticism when told a legend believe it. After all, it is in print. Someone must have verified the fact.

In between oral transmission and published sources is the world of quasi-publication. In days past, this consisted mainly of photocopied and faxed distribution. Now, of course, we have the internet. Both traditional urban legends—especially those that give warnings about things like poisoned Halloween candy or stolen kidneys—as well as linguistic ones thrive in these media.

E-mail provides a way for people to pass on interesting tales and tidbits of information. Hoaxes like the "Life in the 1500s" story (chapter 2, p. 61) used to be confined to faxes and to photocopies pinned to lunchroom bulletin boards. Now they circle the globe at the speed of light to thousands of new readers every day.

Websites that discuss these legends have sprung up. Some are quite excellent, providing well-researched and documented information. Others are not as good. Unfortunately, search engines like Google do not display their search results in order of accuracy, with the most reliable information first. That would be an impossible feat. Rather, they typically give the results in order of the popularity of the websites. Popularity, unfortunately, does not strongly correlate with accuracy.

The web has also opened up whole new sources of false information to ordinary people. Some linguistic legends are particularly prevalent in certain fields. The Chevy Nova/No Go legend, for example, is very common in the field of international marketing. One finds it in advertising and promotional literature for translation and localization services. Business journals carry columns and articles that cite it as an example of what not to do. Even marketing textbooks print the legend as fact. Most people would never encounter these sources if it were not for the web.

Who Tells Them?

We all tell urban legends and the same is true for linguistic urban legends. But there are some groups of people that tend to tell, or vector, linguistic urban legends more than most. These are tour guides, teachers, preachers, and journalists.

What do these four groups have in common that makes them likely vectors for these stories? They tend to speak or write often, usually to large audiences. They address subjects in which they are not necessarily experts. To make their lessons appealing, they incorporate a wide range of material into their lessons and stories. They throw in a linguistic or etymological tidbit here and there to make things interesting.

Journalists are generalists. They write about all sorts of things. Preachers may be expert in the underlying theological premises of their sermons, but the illustrations they use in their sermons and homilies often range far afield from the subjects they studied in seminary. Primary and secondary school teachers are seldom experts in all the fields they have to teach. Even college professors are rarely fully versed in all aspects of their subject, particularly when it comes to introductory classes. Scholarly expertise is usually quite narrow. And tour guides often receive little or no training at all.

Finally, all of these people carry with them authority. We expect them to tell us the truth. Of course, they usually do. As a rule, our trust is not misplaced. The bulk of what they tell us is indeed correct, but with the volume of information and the wide range of subjects they cover, errors are bound to creep in.

Are We Being Spoilsports?

Anyone who has any experience debunking legends or pseudoscience knows that the task is often an unappreciated one. People do not like to have their beliefs questioned or to have good stories spoiled. After all, these are just stories; does it matter if they are not true?

In many cases the answer is probably not much, but these stories do color the way we look at the world. Take the example of the belief that John F. Kennedy's line "Ich bin ein Berliner" means "I am a jelly doughnut" (chapter 7, p. 186). Unless one is studying the nuances of idiomatic German, the underlying linguistic point is probably unimportant. But because of this false legend, many have the impression that people were laughing at Kennedy when he said it. Nothing could be further from the truth. It was an inspiring speech and a masterstroke of rhetoric. In this age of cynicism about American presidents and transatlantic relations, it is easy to forget that in 1963, the American president standing shoulder to shoulder with the people of Berlin was not a laughing matter. It is instructive to remember that not so very long ago the state of diplomatic relations between Western Europe and the United States was a deadly serious matter.

The idea that *rule of thumb* is a reference to the alleged right husbands had to beat their wives (chapter 1, p. 38) is another example of a legend that colors how we look at our world. The legend holds that American and English legal practices have traditionally upheld the right of a man to apply "moderate correction" to his wife. The fact is that for over 400 years, since the beginnings of English Common Law, spousal abuse has been regarded as illegal. To be sure, the law has not always been observed or enforced, but wife beating has never enjoyed official sanction in American or English legal tradition. To suggest otherwise distorts the role that women played in society and covers up and hides the fact that some of the things that feminists have been militating for are not new or radical at all.

Other legends cannot be interpreted as having a negative effect. Does it matter whether or not *hot dog* (chapter 1, p. 58) was coined by cartoonist T. A. Dorgan? Or whether or not the name *Windy City* (chapter 1, p. 54) refers to Chicago politicians? In the great scheme of things, probably not. But in the end, we are better served by knowing the truth, and an awareness of the insidious nature of legends and misinformation can help us avoid false beliefs when they really do matter.

How Do We Ferret Out the Truth?

Every researcher, regardless of the discipline, uses a set of tools to verify facts and make new observations. These tools include such things as literature searches, gas chromatographs, particle accelerators, computer models, and the like. Which tools are used depends on the discipline (a biologist, for example, has little need for a particle accelerator) and on the question being asked.

Linguistics and etymology are no different from the "hard sciences" in this respect, only the tools are different. And unlike in the hard sciences, even the amateur skeptic has readily available many of the tools needed to debunk linguistic urban legends. Furthermore, debunking most of these legends does not require a great deal of linguistic expertise. All that is required are critical thinking skills and a good dictionary. So before we venture into the legends themselves, we should take a look at some of the tools used to debunk them.

Historical Dictionaries

Historical dictionaries are large, usually multi-volume affairs. They contain detailed information about the use of words and phrases over the centuries. They also contain actual citations of use, so a researcher can come to her own conclusions about a word or phrase, without relying solely on the judgment of the dictionary editors.

The most famous historical dictionary is the *Oxford English Dictionary* (*OED*). The second edition clocks in at twenty volumes. It is by far the best single source for information on English words and phrases. It is also available online, although not for free. There are others, such as the *Historical Dictionary of American Slang* and the *Dictionary of American Regional English* that are also excellent sources, albeit not as comprehensive as the *OED*.

Standard Dictionaries

The most common and useful etymological tool is a standard dictionary. For those without ready access to a historical dictionary, a standard dictionary will usually suffice. Fortunately, most standard dictionaries are the products of quality research. They do not provide the in-depth detail that historical dictionaries do, but that does not mean they are not useful. Most good dictionaries include etymological information about their entries. Usually, this can be found at the beginning of the entry, immediately following the pronunciation and part of speech classification. Take, for example, this entry from the *Shorter Oxford English Dictionary* (*SOED*):

infantry / inf(ə)ntri/ *noun*. L16.
[French *infanterie* from Italian *infanteria*, from *infante* youth, foot-soldier, from Latin *infant-*; see INFANT *noun*[1], -ERY.]
1. Soldiers marching or fighting on foot; the body of foot-soldiers. L16.
light infantry: see LIGHT *adjective*[1]. **mounted infantry** soldiers who are mounted for transit but who fight on foot.

C.V. WEDGEWOOD Two hundred infantry and forty
horsemen crossed from the mainland to the Isle of Wight.
2. *collect.* Infants. *joc.* E17
M. NEEDHAM The little dirty Infantry, which swarms up
and down in Alleys and Lanes.
Comb.: **infantryman** a soldier of an infantry regiment.

In this entry, we first find the head word, *infantry*, which is
followed by the pronunciation, the part of speech classification—in this case a noun—and the approximate date, the late
sixteenth century, when the word came into English use. This
header information is followed by the etymology, in square
brackets. The etymology is then followed by the definitions; in
this case there are two main senses. Following the definitions,
the *SOED* gives a usage citation for each sense. A single citation like this is not very useful in tracing the etymology.
Rather, it is included here so that we can see how the word is
commonly used in a sentence. Finally, the entry gives us some
compounds and combining forms of the word. The order of
the components of the entry and the abbreviations used will
vary from dictionary to dictionary. Look in the front of the
dictionary to find the style and abbreviations used by that particular set of editors.

In this case, we can see that infantry comes into English from
the French *infanterie*, which in turn comes from the Italian *infanteria*. This Italian military term comes from the word *infante*,
which can mean a child as well as a foot soldier. This Italian
word ultimately comes from the Latin root *infant-*. Finally the
dictionary tells us that there is more information to be found
under the entry for *infant*.

Most standard dictionaries omit the date that a word or phrase entered the language. This tends to be the most serious etymological drawback with standard dictionaries, although some, such as the *SOED* cited here, give a general date.

Etymological Dictionaries

An etymological dictionary is simply one that focuses on the etymological portion of the entry. It will include more details on the origins, such as the dates when various word forms appeared in the language or extended notes on the origins. This is usually done at the sacrifice of other information. Pronunciations, plural and other forms, and sometimes even definitions are abbreviated or left out.

Slang, Jargon, and Dialectal Dictionaries

These are dictionaries that focus on certain subsets of the language. Their advantage is that they include words and phrases that often are not included in standard dictionaries because they are considered nonstandard terms. The chief disadvantage of these dictionaries is that they are not comprehensive, but within their narrow field they are often superior to general dictionaries. A slang dictionary focuses on nonstandard words and phrases. A jargon dictionary, often called a technical dictionary by title, concentrates on words used in certain professional or technical fields, such as the sciences or engineering. A regional or dialectal dictionary attempts to capture the language used in a particular region or dialect. Often these dictionaries omit etymological information, concentrating on the definition.

Popular Press Books

Some popular press books about language and etymology contain wildly inaccurate information. Others are of superb quality. Popular press books tend to focus on slang or "interesting" words and phrases and are rarely useful for most ordinary words (but then that is why we have dictionaries).

The chief drawback of popular press books is that most do not contain source information. This makes them nearly useless as research tools. It is also sometimes difficult to quickly gauge the quality of popular press books. They may have the veneer of sound scholarship, but be filled with inaccuracies that only come to light after extended checking against other sources.

One good way to gauge the quality of a book is to check a standard set of words. I often use *posh, wog*, and *the whole nine yards*. Using these known words and phrases, one can quickly evaluate the accuracy, quantity, and presentation of the information.

Primary Research Tools

The types of books listed above are all you will need to verify or debunk most linguistic urban legends that come your way. But they all have a drawback (even the *OED*) in that they only reflect research that has already been done. The authors and editors summarize the work of those before them. They are "secondary sources."

To go beyond this and push the boundaries of the field, one must use primary materials. You must read actual books, newspapers, and manuscripts looking for the word or phrase in question and listen to tapes of how words are pronounced and used. It is a lengthy and time-consuming endeavor.

Fortunately, we live in a computer age and every day more material is available in computer databases, such as *Lexis-Nexis* and the *Proquest Newspaper Databases*. Unfortunately, many of the most useful services, like the two just mentioned, are expensive and remain the province of professionals. However, others like the Library of Congress's *American Memory* and Cornell's *Making of America* databases are free on the internet.

Most of us, however, do not need to resort to primary source materials. If you simply want to verify a juicy story, usually a dictionary or a well-done Google search will suffice.

chapter /'cHaptər/ One

Debunking the
Big Boys

To begin our exploration of linguistic urban legends, we might as well jump into the deep end. Of the many false linguistic stories floating about out there, some are classics. They keep appearing again and again, spreading without let or hindrance.

While these popular tales do not fit exactly into the mold of a traditional or classic urban legend, they do share many of the same characteristics. These stories just spring up and propagate. They are suggested by friends or appear on websites. They often attach themselves to some cultural phenomenon, referencing such things as death, ethnic pride, and history. And such linguistic legends are usually false, although they may have a grain of truth at the core. A good example is the children's rhyme *Ring Around the Rosie.*

Ring Around the Rosie

We are all familiar with this children's rhyme. In one of its most common forms today (there are many variants), it reads:

Ring around the rosie,
A pocket full of posies,
Ashes, ashes,
We all fall down.

It is a catchy little poem, complete with pantomimes that appeal to children, like walking in circles and falling to the ground at the end. But what does it mean? It seems a bit nonsensical to us adults. This is where the legendary aspect comes in.

The common folkloric explanation is that this is a rhyme about the bubonic plague that killed one third of the population of Europe in the fourteenth century. The key, according to the legend, is in the words. *Ring around the rosie* allegedly refers to buboes on the skin. *A pocket full of posies* refers to flowers kept in one's pocket, from the medieval belief that pleasant odors would ward off the disease. *Ashes, ashes* is a reference to either mass cremations or to the line from the funeral service, "ashes to ashes, dust to dust." Often, the third line reads *atishoo, atishoo,* in which case it is said to be a reference to sneezing, an early indicator of the plague's pneumonic form. Finally, *fall down* is a child's representation of death.

A neat tale. It fits the definition of an urban legend almost to a tee. The story has no definite point of origin. There is no scholarly paper that advances the argument and provides evidence of the rhyme's origin in the Black Death. And it has an element of horror—the plague. And it is quite untrue.

The legend appeals to a perverse mentality that uses the innocence of childhood to conceal a horrible tragedy. (If only the children understood the poem they were so ritualistically chanting . . .) It also taps into the mythic theme of a collective consciousness that remembers past events. The idea of a sub-rosa literary theme that comes down through the ages is appealing. This is good stuff on many levels and it is no wonder that the tale is a popular one. Unfortunately, there is no evidence to support the story.

Just as a physicist does not claim a hypothesis is true without experimentation and observation, an etymologist does not plump for a story simply because it sounds logical. One must look to the record. When did the poem first appear? Is the modern version of the rhyme the same as the early ones? Do the early versions of the poem also contain viable references to the plague? Were buboes described as "roses" in the medieval accounts of the disease?

There is some theoretical basis for thinking the story might be true. Many nursery rhymes are based on or contain fragments of adult poetry and song. Some do indeed make reference to historical events and occasionally one will be found that has echoes of some centuries-old event. Nursery rhymes were not systematically collected or written down until the mid-eighteenth century and their early history is murky at best. But in the case of *Ring Around the Rosie*, the available evidence does not support the tale.

The rhyme is first published in Kate Greenaway's 1881 *Mother Goose*, some 215 years after the last great plague struck England, and some 550 years after the Black Death of the fourteenth century—the outbreak most commonly associated with the bubonic plague. For the folkloric explanation to be true, the rhyme would have to have remained underground for at least two centuries and then finally appear in the form of a children's nursery rhyme.

There is some evidence to indicate that the rhyme may date to as early as 1790, collapsing this timeline somewhat. If this is true, the rhyme would have been recorded only some 125 years after the Great Plague of 1665. But the alleged 1790 citation also points to an origin in North America, a continent that has never known a major outbreak of the bubonic plague, at least among those of European descent.

But the most convincing evidence against the plague explanation is that the earliest versions of the rhyme are different, and are less subject to the plague interpretation than the versions best known today. The 1881 Greenaway version of the rhyme reads:

> Ring-a-ring o' roses,
> A pocket full of posies,
> Hush! hush! hush! hush!
> We're all tumbled down[1]

This version appears not so much as a story about death and disease, but rather about falling asleep after a day of picking flowers.

A few years after the Greenaway book was published, an American version of the rhyme was recorded in William Wells Newell's 1883 *Games and Songs of American Children*. Newell claims that the following version of the rhyme was common among the children of New Bedford, Massachusetts, ca. 1790:

> Ring a ring a rosie,
> A bottle full of posie,
> All the girls in our town
> Ring for little Josie.

This one is even less explainable in terms of the plague. Assuming that Newell is correct and that this version does indeed date to 1790, it seems that the further back we go, the less tenable the plague explanation becomes.

Newell also published another version of the rhyme, explaining the "rosie" and "falling down" lines and providing commentary on how the children played the game:

> Round the ring of roses,
> Pots full of posies,
> The one who stoops last
> Shall tell whom she loves best.

Newell comments: "At the end of the words the children suddenly stoop, and the last to get down undergoes some penalty, or has to take the place of the child in the centre, who represents the 'rosie' (rose-tree; French, rosier)."[2]

There are many other early variants. In her 1894–98 work *The Traditional Games of England, Scotland, and Ireland*, Alice Bertha Gomme collected some twelve different versions of the rhyme. Of these, only one is similar to the modern version that is the subject of the plague interpretation.

And was the word *rose* or *rosie* ever used to refer to buboes caused by the plague? Not according to the *Oxford English Dictionary*. There is no known use of the words in reference to plague. *The Rose* is an archaic name for the skin disease erysipelas, most often found among butchers and those who gut fish for a living, but this is a minor skin condition, a far cry from plague.[3]

So if it is not about the plague, what is it about? Most likely it is simply nonsense, like *Hickory, Dickory, Dock* or *The cow jumped over the moon*. Who says children's rhymes have to make sense to us adults?

The need to make sense of words with arcane origins is a common motivator behind etymological legends. These are not confined to the realm of children's rhymes, but can also be about some of the most common terms in our everyday vocabulary. A classic example is *OK*.

OK

OK is the most successful of all Americanisms. It has invaded hundreds of other languages and been adopted by them as a word. H. L. Mencken claimed that U.S. troops deployed overseas during World War II found it already in use by people around the world, from the Bedouins in the Sahara to the Japanese in the Pacific. It was also the first unscripted word spoken on the surface of the moon, uttered by Buzz Aldrin just after the lunar module touched down.

OK is ubiquitous. Perhaps because it is such a successful word and because it is an abbreviation for something that is not immediately obvious, people want to know where the *OK* comes from. Unlike *Ring Around the Rosie*, however, *OK* did not spawn a single creation myth. Instead, it has spawned dozens of explanations.

Despite the term's success in entrenching itself in American speech, for over a hundred years no one was really sure of the word's origin. The origin of *OK* became the Holy Grail of etymology. Finally, in 1963–64 the Galahad of our story, Allen Walker Read of Columbia University uncovered the origin in a series of articles in the journal *American Speech*.[4]

But before we get to the actual origin, let us take a look at some of the more popular suggestions as to the origin of *OK*. These can all be dismissed due to lack of evidence or because *OK* predates the events that supposedly led to its creation, although the first two come rather close to the truth:

- Andrew Jackson, seventh president of the United States (1829–37), was a terrible speller, nearly illiterate. He misspelled the phrase *all correct* as *oll korrect* and then abbreviated it as *OK*. (In some variants someone else is the bad speller, but Jackson is the most common culprit. Dan Quayle and George W. Bush can take heart—accusing national leaders of linguistic faux pas is practically an American pastime. Cf. John F. Kennedy's "I am a jelly doughnut" in chapter 7, p. 186.)
- It stands for *Old Kinderhook*, the nickname of Martin Van Buren, eighth president of the United States (1837-41), who came from Kinderhook, New York.
- It comes from one of any number of languages:
  - It is from the Choctaw word *okeh*. Often this explanation involves Andrew Jackson again, but this time he adopts the word from the Indian language, not because he is orthographically challenged.
  - It is from the Greek *olla kalla*, meaning all right or satisfactory.
  - It is an abbreviation for the German *Oberst Kommandant*, or Colonel in Command, used by either Generals Von Steuben or Schliessen (take your pick) during the Revolutionary War. No record of either man—or anyone, until 1839, using this phrase—exists.
  - It is from Scottish dialect, *och aye*.
  - It is from the Finnish *oikea*.
  - It is from Ewe, a West African language spoken by some slaves in the American South.
  - It comes from the French *Aux Cayes*, a port in Haiti famed for its rum.
- It stands for *Orrin Kendall* crackers supplied to the Union Army during the Civil War. Unfortunately for Kendall's

immortality, *OK* was in use more than twenty years before the Civil War.

- It stands for *Obadiah Kelly*, a railroad shipping clerk who initialed bills of lading.
- It is from the telegraph term *Open Key*. But again, the telegraph was invented in 1844, after *OK* was in use.

Of the above explanations, the first two are closest to the truth, but still not quite right. Andrew Jackson was a notoriously poor speller. So much so, that his spelling became an issue in the 1828 presidential campaign.[5] He is not, however, known to have ever used the expression *OK* or misspelled *all correct* with the two letters in question. The actual origin has nothing to do with Andrew Jackson, but it is from a misspelling of *all correct*. And Martin "Old Kinderhook" Van Buren did play a major role in the early popularity and spread of the word, but his nickname is not the origin.

Allen Walker Read traced the origin of *OK* to a fad of facetious abbreviations that swept Boston beginning in 1838. In the summer of that year, Boston newspaper editors took to creating abbreviations for various phrases. These included, but were not limited to:

- O.F.M. = Our First Men
- G.T.D.H.D. = Give The Devil His Due
- N.G. = No Go
- S.P. = Small Potatoes

This practice is much the same as what we see on the internet today, where abbreviations such as the following are common:

- ROTFL = Rolling On The Floor Laughing
- IIRC = If I Recall Correctly

- WYSIWYG = What You See Is What You Get
- YMMV = Your Mileage May Vary

Often these Boston editors would deliberately misspell an abbreviation. On June 18, 1838, some nine months before *OK* makes its appearance, the Boston *Morning Post* included the following: "We jumped in, and were not disappointed either with the carriage, distance, or price. It was O.W.—(all right.)"

Clearly, the editor is abbreviating the phrase as if it were spelled *oll wright*. New York papers picked up the practice in the summer of 1838, using *K.G.* for *no go*, *K.Y.* for *no use*, and *K.K.N.* for *commit no nuisance*. (And we still see this type of jocular misspelling today. One example is the joke about how the letter N on the University of Nebraska football helmets stands for "knowledge." Similarly, some colleagues of mine and I formed a group known as the R.O.A.N., or the Repository Of All Knowledge. We claimed that among us we could find the answer to any question and joked that we spelled the name that way because the "K" was silent.)

It is in this tradition that *OK* makes its debut. The date is March 23, 1839, and the paper is again the Boston *Morning Post*. One of the editors penned: ". . . perhaps if he should return to Boston, via Providence, he of the [Providence] Journal, and his *train*-band, would have the "contribution box," et ceteras, *o.k.*—all correct—and cause the corks to fly, like *sparks* upward."

Over the next few weeks and months, the *Morning Post* reused *OK* several times and by September the term had traveled south. The New York *Evening Tattler* first used *OK* on the second of that month. The newspaper abbreviation fad hit New Orleans in October and in November both the fad and *OK* began appearing in Philadelphia papers. The term was off and running.

But *OK* probably would have died the death its cousins *O.F.M.* and *G.T.D.H.D.* did if it were not for another event. In March 1840—exactly a year after *OK* made its Boston debut—New York Democrats formed an organization called the *OK Club*. The name of the club stood for Old Kinderhook as Martin Van Buren was running for reelection that year. Since *OK* was in widespread use prior to the formation of the OK Club, it seems likely that the name of the club was due, at least in part, to the phrase. In choosing the name, Democrats were linking their candidate, Old Kinderhook, with the phrase that meant "all is right."

The 1840 presidential campaign saw widespread use of the initials *O.K.* They appeared on signs, in newspapers, in pamphlets. They were shouted at meetings and conventions across the United States. Old Kinderhook was not the origin of the word, but it was probably what cemented the word's place in American speech.

Others, trying to debunk Read's hypothesis, point to three alleged earlier uses of *OK*. Two of these cases are clearly misreadings of handwritten records and are not actually instances of *OK* at all. The third may be the two letters in question, but if so their meaning is ambiguous.

The first of these alleged uses is a 1757 muster record of the Massachusetts militia where the commander, a David Black, attests that the record is correct. It allegedly reads: "A True Roll OK David Black."

But an examination of the actual document, as opposed to a transcription, clearly shows that the letters *OK* do not appear. Instead it actually reads "Att," a common legal abbreviation of the day for attested or attestor.[6]

The second document is a 1790 court record from Sumner County, Tennessee, that concerns Andrew Jackson—a man who seems to be inextricably linked with the folklore of *OK*. The record involves the sale of a slave in which Jackson "proved a bill of sale from Hugh McGary to Kasper Mansker, for a Negro man, which was O.K." But this is just poor penmanship on the part of a court clerk. The K is actually an R. The document actually reads *O.R.*, which was a common abbreviation in such records, meaning "Order Recorded."[7]

The third document is from an 1815 travel diary of one William Richardson. What appears to be the letters *ok* are interlined in the February 21 entry and appear among several crossed out words and edits. Unlike the other two alleged instances, we cannot quickly dismiss this one as a misreading or poor transcription. The document reads:

> . . . all day. ~~We this day dined~~ Arrived at in Princeton, a handsome little village, 15 miles from N Brunswick, & ^ok^ ~~Arrived~~ & at Trenton, where we dined at 1 P.M.

The letters do indeed appear to be *ok*, but their meaning, if there is a meaning, cannot be deduced. There is no plausible reason why Richardson would write a term meaning "all right" at this point in the document. More likely, the letters are simply a fragment of an incomplete phrase. The evidence points to this being a spurious appearance of the two letters in question and not an early instance of the word we know as *OK*.[8]

When Read solved the mystery of the origin of *OK* in 1963, he seemingly had found the Holy Grail of American etymology. But the 1960s saw the rise of a new phrase that would eventually take the place of *OK* as the greatest etymological mystery. By the end of the twentieth century, this other phrase was attracting a mass of explanations; only this time, the origin remains a mystery still.

The Whole Nine Yards

Nine yards of what? That is the great question. The correct answer is a bit disappointing: no one knows. But that does not stop people from promulgating answers. These alleged origins include:

- It is a reference to American football, albeit used sarcastically. To go the "whole nine yards" is to come up one yard short of a first down.
- It is the amount of cloth needed to make
  - A kilt
  - A sari
  - A man's suit
  - A bridal veil
  - A sarong
  - A kimono
  - A burial shroud
- The length of a belt of machine-gun ammunition carried in a World War II fighter plane.
- The number of cubic yards of concrete carried in a concrete mixing truck.
- The number of cubic yards of coal in a coal truck.
- The number of cubic yards of dirt in a burial plot.
- The number of yardarms on a square-rigged sailing vessel.
- The number of lots in a New York City block (or Philadelphia or Levittown or fill in your choice city).

Before we start to pick these explanations apart, let us look at what we know about the phrase. First, the phrase is not nearly as old as most people think. The earliest known use of *the whole nine yards* is only from 1966. It appears in Elaine Shepard's novel *Doom Pussy*, about U.S. Air Force pilots in

Vietnam: "The first thing in the early pearly morning and the last thing at night. Beds all over the gahdam [sic] house. The whole nine yards."[9]

There is an intriguing use of *nine yards* from a few years earlier, though. In November 1958, Manly Wade Wellman published a poem in *The Magazine of Fantasy & Science Fiction* titled *Nine Yards of Other Cloth* that references the traditional length of a burial shroud in Appalachian custom. The relevant passage reads:

I'll weave nine yards of other cloth
For John to have and keep,
He'll need it where he's going to lie,
To warm him in his sleep.[10]

So we have two clues here, but neither passage points to a definitive origin. The 1966 quotation uses the phrase in the common sense, meaning the whole, everything. The source is slang used by airmen in Vietnam, but this does not necessarily mean that the origin is in Air Force jargon. The airmen could just as easily have picked up the phrase from the civilian world.

The 1958 citation is interesting, but the poem does not use the word *whole*, nor does it use the phrase *nine yards* to indicate the entirety of something. It is a literal reference to nine yards of cloth. There are thousands, if not millions, of such references to nine yards of something or other. In all these cases they are simply literal references to measurements that just happen to be nine yards. The length has no significance beyond the literal measurement. So while it looks interesting, we cannot say that the phrase's origin lies in Appalachian funeral practices. These quotes point out two areas that might be fruitful places to look for early uses of *the whole nine yards*, namely

military aviation and Appalachian funeral traditions, but neither offers a definitive origin.

An explanation that gained currency among many self-pro-
fessed language experts, notably newspaper columnists William
Safire and James Kilpatrick, was the concrete truck explanation. This explanation, however, is certainly false. The numbers
just do not add up. The August 1964 issue of *Ready Mixed
Concrete* magazine gives the following figures:

> The trend toward larger truck mixer units is probably one of
> the strongest and most persistent trends in the industry.
> Whereas, just a few years ago, the 4 1/2 cubic yard mixer was
> definitely the standard of the industry, the average nation-
> wide mixer size by 1962 had increased to 6.24 cubic yards,
> with still no end in sight to the demand for increased pay-
> load.[11]

While today's concrete mixers may have capacities of nine cubic yards, back when the phrase came into use they were much
smaller. So the concrete truck explanation is almost certainly
incorrect.

Similarly, the "amount of cloth it takes to make a . . ." explanations are also without merit. First, there is no standard size
for a bolt of cloth, which usually measures anywhere from
twenty to twenty-five yards and widths vary similarly. So to say
one wants "nine yards of cloth" is a very inexact statement.
Also, nine yards is not a significant measure for any type of garment. Most garments will use varying amounts of cloth, depending on quality, cut, size of the individual, etc. There is no
such standard for the tailoring of any garment.

The explanation of yards, or lots, to the city block shares a
similar problem regarding standardization. There simply is no
standard lot size. Lots can vary within the same city or even the

same neighborhood. Also, the lengths of city blocks change as well. And the fact that the city in question changes with the telling is a dead giveaway that we are dealing with an urban legend. It is never the city that we are in, so we cannot go outside and start counting. It is always another city, too far away to easily verify how many yards are in each block, where the phrase got its start.

Ditto for the sailing ship explanation. The number of yards on a square-rigged vessel is not fixed at nine. Depending on the ship and how she is rigged, there can be more or less. But even more damning is the date. A phrase from the 1960s is unlikely to have originated in the Age of Sail.

As to the amount of dirt in a burial plot, nine cubic yards would be an awfully big grave. Most plots only contain about four cubic yards of dirt.

One explanation that appeared on the internet a few years back and has gained widespread currency of late is that *the whole nine yards* refers to the length of a belt of machine-gun ammunition carried by a World War II fighter plane. To "give it the whole nine yards" was to expend all of one's ammo. Despite the 1966 *Doom Pussy* quotation, which indicates the phrase might have an origin in military aviation, this explanation is almost certainly false. For one thing, the type of fighter varies with the telling, sometimes Spitfires in the Battle of Britain, sometimes different types of American fighters in the South Pacific. And there are no citations of use from WWII. With the wealth of literature, letters, news reports, etc. that came out of the war, one would think the phrase would have appeared earlier than 1966 if it had a World War II origin. Finally, perhaps the best reason to question this explanation is that ammunition is either counted in rounds or measured by weight. It is never measured by the length of a belt.

Finally unlike most of the others, the football explanation is
eminently plausible. But again there is that pesky problem with
evidence. It is not enough just to have a hypothesis that is plausible. We also require some early use of the phrase linking it to
football before we can buy into it.

So, in the end we are left with a bunch of debunked explanations and a conclusion of "origin unknown." Not very satisfying, but that is often the way with etymological research.
There is some hope though. Those early quotes give us a couple of areas to look into for other uses of *the whole nine yards*.
Perhaps some future etymologist will channel Allen Walker
Read and discover the true origin.

Rule of Thumb

Some legends are propagated because the moral lesson underlying them supports a political agenda. Members of special-
interest groups repeat the tale because it fits their purpose.
While such people usually do not set out to deliberately distort
facts and tell untruths, neither are they particularly motivated
to investigate deeply to determine if the tale they are telling is
true. Such is the case with feminists and the phrase *rule of
thumb*. Take this quote from a standard women's studies text-
book: "The popular expression 'rule of thumb' originated from
English common law, which allowed a husband to beat his wife
with a whip or stick no bigger in diameter than his thumb. The
husband's prerogative was incorporated into American law.
Several states had statutes that essentially allowed a man to beat
his wife without interference from the courts."[12]

Modern folklore would have it that the phrase *rule of
thumb* is from English common law. This story, unlike many
linguistic urban legends, has a true element of horror. It pur-

ports to demonstrate how modern civilization is not much more than a thin veneer over our more brutal tendencies. A seemingly innocuous phrase has roots in man's more primitive and brutal past.

It was true in some places (and unfortunately still is in too many) that men were permitted to beat their wives, but this rule was never codified in English legal tradition; and a rule limiting such beating to sticks of a particular size never existed. In fact, this story of the phrase's origin does not appear until the 1970s. Nor are the claims backed up with actual citations of legal precedent. Needless to say, this mythical rule is not the basis for the everyday expression.

Wife beating in English (and American) legal tradition has a mixed history. Officially, wife beating has been illegal for hundreds of years and often punishable by stiff penalties; but enforcement of the law has too often been problematic, and some judges have allowed a marriage license to be admitted as mitigating evidence in assault cases. Blackstone in his classic *Commentaries on the Laws of England* (1765) acknowledges, but does not support this latter view:

> The husband also (by the old law) might give his wife moderate correction. [. . .] But this power of correction was confined within reasonable bounds; and the husband was prohibited to use any violence to his wife, *aliter quam ad virum, ex causa regiminis et castigationis uxoris suae, licited et rationabiliter pertinet* (other than what is reasonably necessary to the discipline and correction of the wife). The civil law gave the husband the same, or a larger, authority over his wife; allowing him, for some misdemeanors, *flagellis et fustibus acriter verbare uxorem* (to wound his wife severely with whips and fists); for others, only *modicam castigationem adhibere* (to apply modest corrective punishment). But, with

us, in the politer reign of Charles the second, this power of correction began to be doubted, and a wife may now have security of the peace against her husband; or, in return, a husband against his wife. Yet the lower rank of people, who were always fond of the old common law, still claim and exert their ancient privilege, and the courts of law will still permit a husband to restrain a wife of her liberty, in case of any gross misbehavior.[13]

Blackstone agrees that in times past, a man might give his wife "moderate correction," but that by the late seventeenth century (the reign of Charles II) this was no longer the case, even if some believed it was. He makes no mention of thumbs or the size of the instrument of said correction.

To our modern, enlightened ears this seems rather brutal, and it was equally brutal to many who lived in the seventeenth and eighteenth centuries. The Massachusetts Bay Colony, for example, prohibited spousal beatings in 1655, five years before Charles II restored the monarchy to England and more than a century before Blackstone wrote his commentary. This early American law read: "No man shall strike his wife nor any woman her husband on penalty of such fine not exceeding ten pounds for one offense, or such corporal punishment as the County shall determine."[14]

By 1870, almost all states had laws prohibiting wife beating, some with penalties that were quite severe, such as forty lashes with a whip or multiple-year imprisonment. And throughout most of the nineteenth century, it was common for wife-beaters to be punished under assault and battery laws.[15]

Legal debates and rulings on the permissibility of wife beating have been found as far back as 1608 and in all these legal opinions or commentaries there are only three that mention thumbs at all. These cases are all American, not English, and date to the nineteenth century. *Bradley v. Mississippi* (1824) upholds the doctrine of beating one's wife with a stick smaller than a thumb:

> I believe it was in a case before Mr. Justice Raymond, where the same doctrine was recognized, with proper limitations and restrictions well suited to the condition and feelings of those who might think proper to use a whip or rattan, no bigger than my thumb, in order to enforce the salutary restraints of domestic discipline.[16]

This Justice Raymond is probably Lord Robert Raymond, a judge on the King's Bench from 1724 to 1733. Despite the reference in the Mississippi court's ruling, no one has found any of Raymond's rulings that relate to such a doctrine.

In *North Carolina v. A. B. Rhodes* (1868) a jury found

> that the defendant struck Elizabeth Rhodes, his wife, three licks, with a switch about the size of his fingers (but not as large as a man's thumb) without any provocation except some words uttered by her and not recollected by the witness.

The trial judge ruled that since the switch was smaller than a thumb, the defendant was not guilty. The judgment was appealed and upheld, but the appellate court ruled that the judge was wrong in thinking a husband had the right to whip his wife, no matter how small the whip:

> Nor is it true that a husband has a right to whip his wife. And if he had, it is not easily seen how the thumb is the standard of size for the instrument which he may use, as some of the old authorities have said; and in deference to which was his Honor's charge. A light blow, or many light

blows, with a stick larger than the thumb, might produce no injury; but a switch half the size might be so used as to produce death. The standard is the effect produced, and not the manner of producing it, or the instrument used.[17]

Finally, in *North Carolina v. Richard Oliver* (1873) the judge writes:

> we may assume that the old doctrine that a husband had a right to whip his wife, provided he used a switch no larger than his thumb, is not law in North Carolina.[18]

The closest anyone has come to identifying such a rule in Britain is a supposed opinion of Francis Buller, a judge on the English bench from 1778 to 1800. In 1782, Buller opined that a man had the right to beat his wife. He was widely castigated in public and called such epithets as "Judge Thumb." The reaction to Buller's opinion makes it clear that this was not a widely held right. No one has been able to identify the specific case in which Buller rendered this opinion, which indicates that it was probably just a publicly stated opinion and not a judicial decision.

So, what we have is a single English judge who in 1782 opined that a man could beat his wife with a stick narrower than his thumb and a handful of American court opinions that cite this English judge. These are joined by some legal debates on whether a husband can punish his wife. But while these legal writings talk about "moderate correction" and sticks the size of a thumb, none of them speak of a *rule of thumb*. How did the phrase *rule of thumb* become connected with this legal belief?

The first person known to have made this connection was Del Martin, a coordinator of the NOW Task Force on Battered Women, who wrote in 1976:

For instance, the common-law doctrine had been modified to allow the husband "the right to whip his wife, provided that he used a switch no bigger than his thumb"—a rule of thumb, so to speak.[19]

Martin never claimed that the phrase had its origin in wife beating. She only metaphorically connected the two, but within a year feminist writings were touting this as the origin of the phrase:

one of the reasons nineteenth century British wives were dealt with so harshly by their husbands and by their legal system was the "rule of thumb" [. . .] Blackstone saw nothing unreasonable about the wife-beating law. In fact, he believed it to be quite moderate.[20]

Note that this last example completely misstates Blackstone's commentary. Blackstone agreed that wife beating was unreasonable and illegal. His statement about "moderate correction" is descriptive of old laws and not indicative of his own opinion or the laws of his time. Misstatements like this became rife in feminist literature and by 1982 even the U.S. Commission on Civil Rights was misstating the legal history of battered spouses:

American law is built upon the British common law that condoned wife beating and even prescribed the weapon to be used. This "rule of thumb" stipulated that a man could only beat his wife with a "rod not thicker than his thumb."[21]

Whether or not feminist literature is the original source for the linguistic confusion is uncertain. The belief that a man was legally entitled to beat his wife with a stick smaller than his thumb was, as we have seen, a widespread belief since at least the nineteenth century. But there is no record of anyone making a connection between that belief and the phrase *rule of thumb* until the 1970s.

As to the actual origin of the phrase, it is most likely an allusion to the fact that the first joint of an adult thumb measures roughly one inch, quite literally a rule (or ruler) of thumb. Since human dimensions vary from person to person, any measurement so taken would be only a rough approximation and not to be trusted where precision was required. The earliest citation of the phrase *rule of thumb* in the *Oxford English Dictionary* is from Hope's *Fencing-Master* from 1692, centuries before anyone connected wife beating with thumb-sized sticks: "What he doth, he doth by rule of Thumb, and not by Art."[22]

Feminists are not the only group to promulgate linguistic legends for their own purposes. There are others as well. One famous legend is used to demonstrate that a particular regional dialect is just as valid as, and perhaps a bit better than, Standard English.

They Speak Elizabethan English in the Appalachians

Mr. Hicks spoke in a dialect scholars describe as Elizabethan, even Chaucerian.[23]
                                         —*New York Times* Obituary, April 27, 2003

When Ray Hicks, a famed Appalachian folklorist and storyteller, died in the spring of 2003, his *New York Times* obituary claimed that his speech patterns were an archaic holdover from centuries past. The obit even went so far as to claim that this had been verified by unnamed (of course) "dialect scholars." This is an oft-repeated myth, that in some backwoods hollows in Appalachia or the Ozarks there are people who speak like Shakespeare did.

The idea that one speaks a purer form of the language is a compelling one. There is so much talk of the decline of the English language, how bad grammar is coming to dominate modern speech, that it is a matter of pride to speak "the Queen's English," or at least the English of Tom Brokaw.

But what if you come from an area that is noted for its rustic and "ungrammatical" speech? Well in that case, you promote a myth that your rustic dialect is actually a pure form of English from ages past and you associate your dialect with some of the greatest poets of the English language. This is exactly what popular folklore has done with the dialect of the Appalachians.

Zell Miller, U.S. senator from and former governor of Georgia, defends his Appalachian dialect in his autobiography, *The Mountains Within Me*:

It no longer bothers me to be kidded about my mountain expressions. In fact, I have come to regard them as status symbols because who else do we have running around in public life today who speaks the language of Chaucer and Shakespeare as distilled, literally and figuratively, by two centuries of Georgia Mountain usage?

Miller goes on to write:

If Shakespeare could have been reincarnated in nineteenth-century Choestoe [a town in Union County, Georgia], he would have felt right at home. The open fireplaces, spinning wheels, handmade looms, Greek lamps and good, if sometimes ungrammatical, Elizabethan English would all have been quite familiar to the Bard of Avon and, with the exception of having to adapt to homespun clothes, he would have little difficulty assimilating into mountain society.[24]

Miller is not the first to promote this idea that the speech of the backwoods hollows and hills of Appalachia is Elizabethan. In the mid-1960s, the state of North Carolina published a pamphlet for tourists titled *A Dictionary of the Queen's English*, which states:

> To outsiders this sounds strange, even uncultured. But what many North Carolinians do to the King's English was done centuries ago by the Queen.
>
> The correspondence and writings of Queen Elizabeth I and such men as Sir Walter Raleigh, Marlowe, Dryden, Bacon and even Shakespeare are sprinkled with words and expressions which today are commonplace in remote regions of North Carolina.
>
> You hear the Queen's English in the coves and hollows of the Blue Ridge and the Great Smoky Mountains and on the windswept Outer Banks where time moves more leisurely.[25]

Other writings promulgating this myth date back to 1915. The myth has been around for a while.

An alert reader will spot some inconsistencies right away, even without any special knowledge of linguistics or the dialects of the American South. First, where are we talking about? Zell Miller's mountains of Georgia? Or in the mountains of North Carolina? Or is it the Atlantic barrier islands of the Outer Banks? The pattern is familiar: the urban legend happened in the next town over; in Appalachia they speak Elizabethan English in the next hollow over. The exact location, or dialect, cannot be pinned down with any specificity.

With a quick look at a historical timeline, other inconsistencies become readily apparent. Jamestown, the first permanent English settlement in North America, was founded in 1607, four years after Elizabeth I died. So if one wishes to quibble, no settlers in North America ever actually spoke "Elizabethan" English; rather, we are talking about Jacobean English.

But putting aside that semantic quibble, there are bigger problems with the timing. The Southern mountains have only been inhabited by Europeans since about the 1790s. By this date Elizabeth I, Shakespeare, Marlowe, Bacon, and Raleigh had all been dead for almost two centuries. John Dryden had been dead about a hundred years and Geoffrey Chaucer had been dead nearly four hundred years.

Further, the early settlers of Appalachia did not come from the London literary elite represented by these writers. They were predominantly Scotts-Irish, which meant they were Protestants from northern Ireland. They were poor farmers and peasants, many illiterate. Their speech was about as similar to Shakespeare's as a modern Belfast dockworker's is to the speech of today's Queen Elizabeth II.

Now it has to be said that there is nothing wrong with speaking like a Belfast dockworker or a Scotts-Irish farmer. Zell Miller has no reason to be ashamed of the way he speaks. His native dialect is not "ungrammatical"; it just operates under slightly different grammatical rules from those of standard American English. No dialect is inherently superior, or inferior, to another. There is no such thing as "pure" English; the English "language" is really just a bunch of mutually intelligible dialects. We have designated a few of these dialects as "standard," but the choice is arbitrary and largely made because of social and class distinctions, not because of any inherent superiority of those dialects.

Some modes of speech, like the dialects of Appalachia, may be associated with a lower social status, but that does not mean that these ways of speaking are inherently wrong. Rather it is simply reflective of a social prejudice against those who speak differently. These dialects are just different from what is judged to be the standard. And this standard is arbitrary and can change. Some seventy years ago, the speech of educated New Englanders was considered the standard American dialect. If you listen to the speech of American movie actors from the 1930s they will sound vaguely British. This is the speech of upper-class New Englanders in the early twentieth century. Today, the standard has moved westward and down the social ladder, so that middle-class Midwesterners (e.g., South Dakota's Tom Brokaw) set the standard.[26]

But back to Elizabethan speech in the Appalachians. Those who promulgate the myth often point to specific words, pronunciations, or grammatical patterns in Appalachian speech that are found in Shakespeare but not in modern Standard English. Among the most commonly cited to defend this myth are the words *afeard*, meaning afraid, *to learn*, meaning to teach, and *holp*, a past tense of help. All three words appear in Shakespeare, but have been lost to today's Standard English.

Afeard, meaning afraid, was a common form in Elizabethan usage. Shakespeare uses it over thirty times in his corpus. And in today's American dialect, its use is largely confined to the southern midlands. But as late as the first half of the twentieth century, it was found throughout the United States and in various British and Irish dialects as well. Its use in Appalachian dialect is not only not unique, it is not even rare.[27]

Similarly, the use of *to learn*, meaning to teach, is hardly confined to mountain hollows. In American dialect it is found throughout the eastern United States, especially among those with just a grade school education.[28] Its use probably has more to do with the level of education of the speaker than where he or she lives. This transitive use of *to learn* is a natural one; most verbs have both transitive and intransitive meanings and there is no logical reason why *to learn* should not also. But in Standard English the transitive use is not acceptable. This is an idiosyncrasy of the standard dialect that has to be drilled into students by years of schooling. The transitive use of *learn* is also found in various British dialects and was used by accomplished British writers like Wodehouse and Disraeli when they wished to replicate the dialect of the working class.[29] Its use is not regional in nature, or even a holdover of Elizabethan English at all; it is just a grammatical structure that is commonly used by the less educated.

Holp, a past tense form of the verb *to help* that was common in Elizabethan English, has never been widely used throughout the United States. It is distinctly a southernism. But that does not mean that it is restricted to isolated mountain hollows. It can be found from Virginia to Florida and west to Texas, and as far north and west as Missouri. It can also be found in various British dialects.[30]

Dialects and speech patterns from other regions have their own archaic relics that are not found in the Appalachians. There is *hap*, a verb meaning to cover and a noun meaning a blanket or comforter. The verb dates to the fourteenth century and survives only in Scots dialect. As a noun it survives in slightly wider usage, not only in Scotland, but also in the north of England and in Pennsylvania.[31] Another Pennsylvania term is *neb* or *to neb*, meaning a nose or to pry or to nose into another's affairs. The word is one of the oldest in the English language, dating to ca. 725, from an Old English word meaning nose. Again, the term survives only in Pennsylvania and in Scots and northern English dialects.[32] In New England, there is a *flake*, a stand or platform for drying food, especially fish. It is often called a *fish flake*. Again, this is an old term from the fourteenth century that survives in the dialectal speech of regions other than the Appalachians.[33] Despite the existence of terms like this, no one is claiming that people from Pennsylvania or Massachusetts speak like Shakespeare or Chaucer.

All dialects change over time. Most will have some relics of Elizabethan language that have fallen out of use elsewhere. Those that are isolated, like Appalachia, may retain a few more archaisms than dialects that have a lot of contact with the outside world, but even these isolated dialects change. The mountain speech of Appalachia or the Ozarks is no more like Elizabethan English than any other dialect, even if a few words or the occasional grammatical structure are similar.

Still the lure of this legend is strong. Those who speak a nonstandard dialect are often stigmatized. They are viewed by outsiders as rustic and uneducated. It is no surprise that they are attracted to a tale that connects them to a great literary tradition.[34] Sometimes, a particular feature of a language will be cited as an example of some underlying sociological fact. It is not necessarily archaisms that are the key; it can be something else entirely. Such is the case for the number of Eskimo words for snow.

500 Eskimo Words for Snow

The myth is that Eskimos have a large number (50, 100, 500, it varies with the telling) of words for snow.[35] Underlying this myth is the assumption that this, if true, is somehow significant. Part of this assumption is the belief that the number of words for something reflects its sociological importance and affects how one thinks. Another part of the assumption is the common theme in urban legends that foreign cultures are strange and different. Eskimos kiss by rubbing noses. Their wives bestow sexual favors on guests. They set their elderly grandparents adrift on ice floes. So it would not seem strange for them to have odd linguistic customs. Of course, all these beliefs about arctic cultures are false, including the one about language.

But where did this myth start? It began much like a snowball rolling downhill, becoming larger and larger until it was too big to stop. In 1911, anthropologist Franz Boas made casual reference to the "fact" that Eskimos had four root words for snow. Boas made the comment in the context of the observation that so-called "primitive" languages were no such thing. Instead, they were every bit as complex and rich as the languages of industrialized Western nations.[36]

The next person in the chain of events leading to the myth was linguist Benjamin Lee Whorf. One of Whorf's major contributions to the field of linguistics was Sapir-Whorf Hypothesis, named for Whorf and his teacher Edward Sapir. The hypothesis had two main component principles, linguistic determination and linguistic relativity. Linguistic determinism holds that language determines how we think, that how we classify and categorize concepts into words defines our outlook on the world. Linguistic relativity holds that verbal distinctions in one language are not necessarily found in others. Germans or Eskimos, for example, think differently from English-speakers because their language is different.

In a 1940 article, Whorf argued that the number of Eskimo words for snow was evidence of linguistic determination. Whereas English only had one word for snow, Eskimo had seven (Whorf upped Boas's count by three). Whorf argued that Eskimos were capable of greater understanding of arctic weather patterns because they had at their disposal a larger number of words with which to think about the subject. Whorf wrote:

> We have the same word for falling snow, snow on the ground, snow packed hard like ice, slushy snow, wind-driven flying snow — whatever the situation may be. To an Eskimo, this all-inclusive word would be almost unthinkable; he would say that falling snow, slushy snow, and so on, are sensuously and operationally different, different things to contend with; he uses different words for them and for other kinds of snow.[37]

An alert reader, without any knowledge of Native American languages, should be able to spot the glaring flaw in Whorf's logic. The flaw is that Whorf has taken an overly simplistic view of the English language, which has many different words for snow. Falling snow can be *snow, flurries*, or *sleet*. Snow packed hard like ice is *hardpack*. Slushy snow is, obviously, *slush*. Wind-driven, flying snow is a *blizzard*. Other snow words include *frost, flakes, powder, corn, dusting, cornice, drift*, and *avalanche*, to name a few.

Linguistic determination, despite the obvious flaws in Whorf's logic, was quite the popular theory in its day. Perhaps the most familiar example of linguistic determination is the theory behind the language of Newspeak in Orwell's *1984*, where Big Brother was attempting to control thought by restricting the language. But few, if any, linguists today put much credence in a strong form of the Sapir-Whorf hypothesis, although it is certainly valid in a weak form. Our language does play a role in perception and memory. We can make conceptual distinctions more quickly and easily if we have words that neatly correspond to those distinctions. An experienced mountaineer may, for example, be able to visualize the terrain of a climb more easily upon hearing the word *cornice* than someone unfamiliar with the term, but a layman can also visualize it—it may just require a longer description. And we can, for example, more easily remember shades of color that we have a name for than shades that we do not—but it does not mean that we cannot distinguish between colors for which we do not have names. Similarly, linguistic relativism does exist. No two languages are quite the same, but precise and accurate translation is not only possible, it is commonplace. This is attested to by the English language equivalents for the many Eskimo words for snow.

But in its day, Whorf's arguments were taken more seriously and were repeated again and again. In this repetition, the number of Eskimo words for snow increased. Boas had four. Whorf had seven. Soon there were a dozen, then fifty, then one hundred, then two hundred. And so on. So, how many Eskimo words for snow are there? The answer is either a few or a lot, depending on how you count.

The two largest Eskimo language groups, Yup'ik and Inuit, are polysynthetic or agglutinative dialects, meaning that words are formed by combining roots and affixes. So, a few basic roots can generate a large number of "words" or lexemes. For example, in the Inuit West Greenlandic dialect the basic word for sea ice is *siku*. Pack ice is *sikursuit*. An ice field is *sikut iqimaniri*. New ice is *sikuliaq* or *sikurlaaq*. Thin ice is *sikuaq* and melting ice *sikurluk*.[38] All these "words" are created using a single root. Boas's original point back in 1911 was that even with a small number of root words, Eskimos could create a stunningly sophisticated descriptive system. It may be simple in certain respects, but it is hardly primitive.

So, depending on how you define "word," there can be anything from a handful to dozens of Eskimo words for snow (but not 500). Since they are agglutinative languages, Yup'ik and Inuit do not have a large number of "words" for snow, as English speakers understand the term. But they do have a very sophisticated linguistic capability for distinguishing between different types of snow. So at its core, the myth is basically true even if the details are misleading. But is this significant?

The answer is an unqualified *no*. The fact that Yup'ik and Inuit languages have a large number of lexemes for snow is trivial and unremarkable. For each of the Inuit words listed above, there is a fairly simple English language equivalent, such as *pack ice*. The equivalent may not be a single word, but English is as equally adept at expressing the distinctions in types of snow as Inuit or Yup'ik.

Going beyond snow, every specialty field has a large vocabulary for items that are important to that field. Just take the field of dog breeding for example. How many names for types of dogs do we have? (hound, setter, pointer, Doberman, Irish setter, English setter, bulldog, chow, Boston terrier, Rhodesian ridgeback, and on and on until we arrive at the mutt). Any decent carpenter can name a number of different types of hammers (ball, claw, tack, sledge). An oncologist can identify many different types of cancers. How many fonts are on your computer, each of them with a name? The fact that there is a large number of words for a thing does not indicate anything other than the fact that one has stumbled into the specialized jargon of some field.

The conclusion is that yes, even though the details are exaggerated and confused, the legend about Eskimo words for snow is basically true. The Native Americans of the far north have a sophisticated way to express winter weather conditions. But so what? Skiers in the Pocono Mountains of Pennsylvania do as well. This fact is utterly unremarkable. If the Yup'ik and Inuit peoples did not have a large number of ways to express different types of arctic weather conditions, we should be surprised.

Windy City

Tradition . . . sometimes brings down truth that history has let slip, but is oftener the wild babble of the time, such as was formerly spoken at the fireside and now congeals in newspapers. . . .
    —Nathaniel Hawthorne, *The House of the Seven Gables*

When the legend becomes fact, print the legend.
                —James Warner Bellah and Willis Goldbeck,
                        The Man Who Shot Liberty Valence

The origin of Chicago's nickname, *the Windy City*, is more factoid than legend. But it is included here because it illustrates a very important point about urban legends: If they are repeated enough, they become accepted unconditionally as truth.

The legend of *Windy City* is a case where newspapers, among others, consistently repeat the false story, despite the fact that knowledge of the true origin has been available for over fifty years to anyone who even bothered to do a modicum of research. We are talking about respected newspapers like the *Chicago Tribune* and the gray lady herself, the *New York Times*, not supermarket tabloids.[39] The newspapers have fallen into a vicious cycle of citing each other instead of doing independent fact checking. It is an urban legend, but instead of attributing a "friend of a friend," each newspaper attributes it to another paper.

This obtains despite the fact that etymologists have been trying to correct the record for years. The false story has been repeated so often that it has become the unquestioned "truth." Even when the error is pointed out, the papers have chosen to go the route of the newspaper editor in *The Man Who Shot Liberty Valence* and "print the legend" instead of the facts.

So what is this *Windy City* myth that the newspapers just will not let go of? The story goes that the nickname for Chicago was coined in 1890 by Charles Dana, the editor of the *New York Sun*. Chicago was competing with New York to host the 1893 Columbian Exposition, and Dana allegedly used the name as a derogatory moniker for the competition. Supposedly the term is not a reference to the winds off Lake Michigan as one might suppose, but rather refers to the Chicagoan habit of rabid boosterism and shameless boasting. To a New Yorker like Dana, Chicago was full of hot air, hence the *Windy City*.

That the story is false is not exactly new information. Mitford Mathew's classic *Dictionary of Americanisms*, published over fifty years ago and long a standard reference book for American slang, includes a citation of *Windy City* from 1887, three years before the fight with New York over hosting the exposition and Dana's alleged coining of the phrase. The same citation is repeated in the *Oxford English Dictionary*.[40] Anyone who did the least bit of research on the term would have discovered the

Dana story to be untenable. In recent years, etymologist Barry Popik has found even earlier uses of the nickname, pushing the coinage back to 1877. The earliest use of *Windy City* that Popik has found is a headline in the *Cincinnati Enquirer* of 12 February 1877: "Gossip and Impressions of the Windy City."[41]

References to the winds off Lake Michigan are even older. Another *Cincinnati Enquirer* article, this one from March 8, 1875, refers to Chicago as the "Municipality of Wind." And these references to Chicago's winds are not limited to the Cincinnati paper. In January 1879, the *Brooklyn Eagle* includes the headline that explains why Chicago is the *Windy City*: "CHICAGO: THE WINDSWEPT CITY OF THE WESTERN PLAINS." It is clear from these and other early citations that the term is indeed from the winds that blow off the lake, not from boosterism or boasting.[42]

Further, Popik's research shows that the nickname was well established by the 1880s, appearing in any number of newspapers across the United States long before Dana allegedly coined it in 1890. So Dana cannot even be credited with popularizing the term.

Finally, there is one last damning problem with the Dana story. Dana may never have even used the phrase *Windy City* at all. Popik, who has exhaustively researched the term, has not found the editorial in question. Not a single account of Dana's alleged coining gives a traceable citation. The 1890 date is simply an assumption based on when Chicago was awarded the Columbian Exposition.[43] It seems likely, however, that Dana did in fact use the phrase but that the citation has been lost, rather than the story being made entirely of whole cloth.

So is there a lesson here other than not to believe everything you read in the newspaper? The real lesson is to be skeptical about your sources of information. Certain sources may be good for certain types of information, but not for others.

Newspaper reporters are not researchers. If they find two or three sources that confirm an alleged fact, they will run with it. Reporters almost exclusively rely on "authorities" to confirm or refute factual evidence. While this is necessary for reporting facts that were personally witnessed and it is often useful when one is short of time or otherwise unable to do the research oneself, it is a poor evidentiary technique in general. Arguments from authority are a rather unreliable form of evidence. Both reporters and the authorities they consult are often duped by folkloric explanations. When it is available, physical evidence is always preferred to an argument from authority.

When investigating an etymological claim, one should not rely on what an authority says, but rather one should go to the actual evidence of use. This is why dictionaries like the *Oxford English Dictionary* include usage citations that show the development of words and phrases. One does not have to rely on the dictionary editor to tell you what the origin is; one can see it for oneself. Thus my extensive footnotes in this book—you do not have to take my word, you can follow the chain of evidence to the source.

It is a question of using the proper research tool. Newspapers are invaluable sources for checking facts about events of the day, but they are not good sources for general facts, like the origins of words and phrases. For that, one must find another source. One must use the right tool, in this case a good historical dictionary—the right tool for the right job. Just as a carpenter does not use a screwdriver to hammer a nail, one should not trust etymologies that are given in newspaper articles.

Windy City is not the only word origin that newspapers are fond of getting wrong. Every Fourth of July sees numerous newspaper articles giving a false etymology to the term *hot dog*.

Hot Dog

There are many stories about the origin of the term hot dog, most of them false. Let us start with what we know. The first known use of the term is in the *Yale Record* of October 19, 1895, which contains the sentence:

> They contentedly munched hot dogs during the whole service.

Two weeks earlier, on October 5, that same paper recorded:

> But I delight to bite the dog
> When placed inside the bun.[44]

The reason why they are called *hot* is obvious, but why *dog*? It is a reference to the alleged contents of the sausage. The association of sausages and dog meat goes back quite a bit further. The term *dog* has been used as a synonym for sausage since at least 1884:

> A sausage maker . . . is continually dunning us for a motto. The following, we hope, will suit him to a hair: "Love me, love my dog."

Citations accusing sausage-makers of using dog meat date to at least 1845:

> Dogs . . . they retails the latter, tails and all, as sassenger meat.[45]

Farmer and Henley's slang dictionary, published in 1891, records *dogs* as university slang for sausages, along with the synonyms *bags of mystery* and *chambers of horrors*.[46] So *hot dog* is simply an extension of the older use of *dog* to mean a sausage.

The most persistent false story about the origins of *hot dog* is the one concerning sausage vendor Harry Stevens, cartoonist Thomas Aloysius "Tad" Dorgan, and the Polo Grounds. According to myth, ca. 1900 Stevens was selling the new snack at a New York Giants baseball game. Dorgan recorded the event in a cartoon, labeling the sausages *hot dogs* because he did not know how to spell *frankfurter*. A variant has Stevens naming the delicacy and Dorgan recording it. Unfortunately, the dates do not work. Not only was the term *hot dog* in use before 1900, but Dorgan was living and drawing in San Francisco in 1900. He did not move to New York City until 1903. Furthermore, no one has found the Dorgan cartoon in question. There are a couple of 1906 Dorgan cartoons featuring hot dogs at a sporting event, but besides being even later, they are from a bicycle race at Madison Square Garden, not a baseball game at the Polo Grounds.[47]

So, while Dorgan did feature hot dogs in a few of his cartoons, he was not the originator of the term. Neither was Harry Stevens or any other food vendor. Nor is the name of the sausage related in any way to the Dachshund breed of dog, another commonly presented false etymology. Yet, like Windy City, newspaper reporters and editors are fond of repeating the legends about the origin of *hot dog* and ignoring the facts.

Journalists are not the only ones fond of repeating linguistic urban legends. All of us are guilty of promulgating these stories. Usually we do this orally, chatting with friends, conversing at cocktail parties, in formal speeches and presentations. One new avenue for ordinary people to promulgate these legends is the internet, a tool that puts publishing power in the hands of almost anyone who wants it. The next chapter deals with just this, an infamous e-mail hoax.

The Elizabethan
E-mail Hoax

One mode of urban legend transmission is known as Xerox®-lore or fax-lore. These are photocopied or faxed accounts of an urban legend. Xerox®-lore and fax-lore are often warnings about particular dangers that we supposedly face in our modern life. Perhaps the most famous are the photocopied warnings about "Blue Star acid," blotter LSD printed with a symbol of a blue star or an image of Mickey Mouse and allegedly distributed in schoolyards. Oral legends change with the telling, mutating to suit local conditions (e.g., the story always takes place in the next town over), but Xerox®-lore is fixed. Once it is distributed, it tends to propagate without change or mutation.

Just as the technologies of photocopiers and facsimile machines added new ways to spread urban legends, so too do the new technologies of the internet. With the advent of mass access

to the internet, beginning around 1994, a new channel of propagating urban legends opened up—e-mail. Legends are copied
and sent to all one's acquaintances at the press of a few buttons.
While e-mail makes changes possible, e-mail warnings tend to
be as static and unchanging as photocopies. Copying and past-
ing the entire legend or hitting the forward button is so much
easier than retelling the tale in one's own words. As a result,
most e-mail-lore works like Xerox-lore, only faster and easier.
Like its technological predecessors, the subject of e-mail-lore
tends toward warnings about the dangers of modern life, such
as computer viruses, missing kidneys, and the like. But every
now and then someone creates a tale about words and language.

   One such tale began making the rounds on the internet back
in 1999. Titled *Life in the 1500s*, it is a prime example of internet
folklore. It continues in circulation today in pretty much the
same form. It is fiction, but before we get into debunking the
details, read it yourself (complete with the original spelling,
grammar, and punctuation errors):

> Anne Hathaway was the wife of William Shakespeare. She
> married at the age of 26. This is really unusual for the time.
> Most people married young, like at the age of 11 or 12. Life
> was not as romantic as we may picture it. Here are some ex-
> amples:
>   Anne Hathaway's home was a 3 bedroom house with a
> small parlor, which was seldom used (only for company),
> kitchen, and no bathroom.
>   Mother and Father shared a bedroom. Anne had a queen
> sized bed, but did not sleep alone. She also had 2 other sis-
> ters and they shared the bed also with 6 servant girls. (this is
> before she married) They didn't sleep like we do length-wise
> but all laid on the bed cross-wise.

At least they had a bed. The other bedroom was shared by her 6 brothers and 30 field workers. They didn't have a bed. Everyone just wrapped up in their blanket and slept on the floor. They had no indoor heating so all the extra bodies kept them warm.

They were also small people, the men only grew to be about 5' 6" and the women were 4' 8". SO [*sic*] in their house they had 27 people living.

Most people got married in June. Why? They took their yearly bath in May, so they were till [*sic*] smelling pretty good by June, although they were starting to smell, so the brides would carry a bouquet of flowers to hide their b.o.

Like I said, they took their yearly bath in May, but it was just a big tub that they would fill with hot water. The man of the house would get the privilege of the nice clean water. Then all the other sons and men, then the women and finally the children. Last of all the babies. By then the water was pretty thick. Thus, the saying, "don't throw the baby out with the bath water," it was so dirty you could actually lose someone in it.

I'll describe their houses a little. You've heard of thatch roofs, well that's all they were. Thick straw, piled high, with no wood underneath. They [*sic*] were the only place for the little animals to get warm. So all the pets; dogs, cats and other small animals, mice, rats, bugs, all lived in the roof. When it rained it became slippery so sometimes the animals would slip and fall off the roof. Thus the saying, "it's raining cats and dogs,"

Since there was nothing to stop things from falling into the house they would just try to clean up a lot. But this posed a real problem in the bedroom where bugs and other droppings from animals could really mess up your nice clean

bed, so they found if they would make beds with big posts
and hang a sheet over the top it would prevent that problem. That's where those beautiful big four poster beds with
canopies came from.

When you came into the house you would notice most
times that the floor was dirt. Only the wealthy had something other than dirt, that's where the saying "dirt poor"
came from. The wealthy would have slate floors. That was
fine but in the winter they would get slippery when they got
wet. So they started to spread thresh on the floor to help
keep their footing. As the winter wore on they would just
keep adding it and adding it until when you opened the
door it would all start slipping outside. SO [*sic*] they put a
piece of wood at the entry way, a "thresh hold".

In the kitchen they would cook over the fire, they had a
fireplace in the kitchen/parlor, that was seldom used and
sometimes in the master bedroom. They had a big kettle
that always hung over the fire and every day they would
light the fire and start adding things to the pot.

Mostly they ate vegetables, they didn't get much meat.
They would eat the stew for dinner then leave the leftovers
in the pot to get cold overnight and then start over the next
day. Sometimes the stew would have food in it that had
been in there for a month! Thus the rhyme: peas [*sic*] porridge hot, peas porridge cold, peas porridge in the pot nine
days old."

Sometimes they could get a hold on [*sic*] some pork.
They really felt special when that happened and when company came over they even had a rack in the parlor where
they would bring out some bacon and hang it to show it off.
That was a sign of wealth and that a man "could really bring
home the bacon." They would cut off a little to share with
guests and they would all sit around and "chew the fat."

If you had money your plates were made out of pewter. Sometimes some of their food had a high acid content and some of the lead would leach out into the food. They really noticed it happened with tomatoes. So they stopped eating tomatoes, for 400 years.

Most people didn't have pewter plates though, they all had trenchers, that was a piece of wood with the middle scooped out like a bowl. They never washed their boards and a lot of times worms would get into the wood. After eating off the trencher with worms they would get "trench mouth." If you were going traveling and wanted to stay at an Inn they usually provided the bed but not the board.

The bread was divided according to status. The workers would get the burnt bottom of the loaf, the family would get the middle and guests would get the top, or the "upper crust".

They also had lead cups and when they would drink their ale or whiskey. [*sic*] The combination would sometimes knock them out for a couple of days. They would be walking along the road and here would be someone knocked out and they thought they were dead. So they would pick them up and take them home and get them ready to bury. They realized if they were too slow about it, the person would wake up. Also, maybe not all of the people they were burying were dead. So they would lay them out on the kitchen table for a couple of days, the family would gather around and eat and drink and wait and see if they would wake up. That's where the custom of holding a "wake" came from.

Since England is so old and small they started running out of places to bury people. So they started digging up some coffins and would take their bones to a house and re-use the grave. They started opening these coffins and found some had scratch marks on the inside.

One out of 25 coffins were that way and they realized they had still been burying people alive. So they thought they would tie a string on their wrist and lead it through the coffin and up through the ground and tie it to a bell. Someone would have to sit out in the graveyard all night to listen for the bell. That is how the saying "graveyard shift" was made. If the bell would ring they would know that someone was "saved by the bell" or he was a "dead ringer".[1]

There are many factual inaccuracies contained in this piece. For example, people in Elizabethan times did not take a single annual bath in May. The account does get some facts right, such as Anne Hathaway's age at marriage; she was 26 and Will was 18 years old. But for the most part, the entire *Life in the 1500s* piece was created out of whole cloth (and nine yards worth at that). I will not attempt to debunk all the cultural and historical inaccuracies, such as bathing practices, but instead will focus on the etymological claims in the piece.

Throw the Baby Out with the Bathwater

The man of the house would get the privilege of the nice clean [bath] water. Then all the other sons and men, then the women and finally the children. Last of all the babies. By then the water was pretty thick. Thus, the saying, "don't throw the baby out with the bath water," it was so dirty you could actually lose someone in it.

Does *throw the baby out with the bathwater* refer to reused wash water that was so dark one could lose a baby in it? Is it Elizabethan in origin? The phrase in question does happen to date to the 1500s, but to Germany, not England; the rest of the story about babies and bathwater is pure fancy.

Throw the baby out with the bathwater (or more accurately, *das Kind mit dem Bade ausschütten*) is a German proverb that dates to 1512. It was first recorded by Thomas Murner in his satire *Narrenbeschwörung* (Appeal to Fools), in which he uses it as a chapter title. Murner uses the phrase several times in the chapter and the original manuscript even has a woodcut of a woman tossing a baby out with the wastewater.

Despite its being a common catchphrase in German (used by such notables as Luther, Kepler, Goethe, Bismarck, Mann, and Grass), the phrase does not appear in English for several more centuries, not until Thomas Carlyle translated it and used it in an 1849 essay on slavery: "And if true, it is important for us, in reference to this Negro Question and some others. The Germans say, 'you must empty-out the bathing-tub, but not the baby along with it.' Fling-out your dirty water with all zeal, and set it careering down the kennels; but try if you can keep the little child!"[2] Carlyle, a Germanophile, is clearly translating the proverb here, using it as a call to not let the slave suffer in the fight to rid the world of the evils of slavery.

And by the way, there is no evidence that anyone ever actually tossed out a baby with the bathwater, in Germany or elsewhere; it is simply evocative and, at least in English, alliterative imagery.

Raining Cats and Dogs

So all the pets; dogs, cats and other small animals, mice, rats, bugs, all lived in the [thatched] roof. When it rained it became slippery so sometimes the animals would slip and fall off the roof. Thus the saying, "it's raining cats and dogs."

Did animals live among the thatch of Elizabethan roofs and then come tumbling down during rainstorms? Sure, mice, rats, and all sorts of insects would make their homes in the thatch of roofs. Perhaps you might find the occasional cat that climbed up after the mice and rats. But dogs? It does not even pass the laugh test.

If one does a little digging, one finds that the phrase *raining cats and dogs* does not even appear until well after the sixteenth century had drawn to a close. Its first recorded use in its modern form is by Jonathan Swift in *Polite Conversation*, written circa 1708 and published thirty years later. This work of Swift is a satire on the use of clichés and the phrase, or at least the metaphor, was in use for a considerable period before this.

The metaphor of the traditional enmity between cats and dogs symbolizing strife and discord does date to Elizabethan times. Stephen Gosson's *The Schoole of Abuse*, written in 1579 contains the following line: "He . . . shall see them agree like Dogges and Cattes."

But the connection to rainstorms does not appear until well after the Elizabethan era. Henry Vaughn's *Olor Iscanus* (1651) includes the lines:

> The Pedlars of our age have business yet,
> And gladly would against the Fayr-day fit
> Themselves with such a Roofe, that can secure
> Their Wares from Dogs and Cats rain'd in showre.

And Richard Brome's *The City Wit* (1652) contains a variant using polecats instead of felines: "It shall raine . . . Dogs and Polecats."[3]

If the phrase has nothing to do with thatch roofs, where does it come from? There are several proposed candidates for why cats and dogs are used to symbolize a heavy rain:

- It is a corruption of the archaic French word *catdoupe*, meaning waterfall or cataract.
- A hard rain would drown cats and dogs in the London streets and in the aftermath it would look as if the animals had fallen from the sky. This explanation is a bit more plausible than animals falling from thatched roofs, especially considering the inadequacies of early London sewers. Again we turn to Jonathan Swift who wrote in his 1710 poem *A Description of a City Shower*:

> Drowned puppies, stinking sprats, all drenched in mud,
> Dead cats and turnip-tops come tumbling down the flood.

- The phrase is an allusion to Norse mythology, in which cats had an influence on the weather, and Odin, the sky god, was attended to by wolves. This would seem unlikely given the late date of the phrase's appearance and none of the early poetic usages make other references to Norse myths.
- A storm is akin to the sound of a cat-and-dog fight.

Occam's Razor would favor the last explanation; it is the simplest and the metaphor corresponds with the early use of cats and dogs to symbolize strife and fighting. A cat-and-dog fight could easily serve as a metaphor for a storm or hard rain.

Dirt Poor

Only the wealthy had something other than dirt, that's where the saying "dirt poor" came from.

Life in the 1500s is not even close with the origin for the term *dirt poor*. For one thing, the term is American in origin. For

another, it only dates to 1937. The original reference is a bit uncertain, but it is most likely evocative of the Dust Bowl and the
extreme poverty in which many had to live during the Depres-
sion or other hardscrabble times.[4]

Threshold

So they started to spread thresh on the floor to help keep
their footing. As the winter wore on they would just keep
adding it and adding it until when you opened the door it
would all start slipping outside. SO [sic] they put a piece of
wood at the entry way, a "thresh hold".

The problem with this explanation for the origin of *threshold* is
that there is no such thing as *thresh*, or at least there was not in
sixteenth-century England. In Scots dialect, there is a plant
called *thresh*, a variant name for the rush. But even this dialectal noun does not appear until 1697. There is a verb, *to thresh*,
meaning to beat cereal plants to separate the grain from the
chaff, but no corresponding noun.

Threshold, on the other hand, is a very old word, dating to
ca. 1000. The first part of the word comes from the verb *to
thresh* originally meant to stamp on or trample and survives today in the verbs *to thresh* (wheat) and *to thrash*. The *hold* portion
is of unknown origin.[5] The *threshold* is literally the first place
you step in a building and has evolved to mean any gateway.

Pease Porridge

Mostly they ate vegetables, they didn't get much meat.
They would eat the stew for dinner then leave the leftovers

in the pot to get cold overnight and then start over the next day. Sometimes the stew would have food in it that had been in there for a month! Thus the rhyme: peas [*sic*] porridge hot, peas porridge cold, peas porridge in the pot nine days old.

Well, everyone gets lucky from time to time. They actually got parts of this one right. Despite the misspelling of *pease*, the dish does date to the sixteenth century and it is a stew that is prepared from leftovers and often is slow cooked over low heat. *Pease porridge* is, however, a stew that contains meat, where the authors imply it is vegetarian.

But while the dish dates to the sixteenth century, the children's rhyme does not, being first recorded in 1797. The rhyme is an imitation of a street hawker's cry, the following version of which was recorded in 1762:

Here's Punch's whole play of the gunpowder-plot, Sir,
With Beasts all alive, and pease-porridge hot, Sir.

Further, the line about the porridge being nine days old is not a reference to how the stew was made. Rather it is a confusion with another street vendor's cry:

Mince pies hot, mince pies cold,
Mince pies in addition nine days old.

So the *pease porridge* poem is simply a conflation of various eighteenth-century street vendors' cries, not the result of unsanitary culinary practices of Elizabethan times.[6] Such conflations are common in children's verse. Children mix and match snippets of adult conversation into rhymes that are phonetically pleasing, but which often make little sense.

Bring Home the Bacon

> . . . they even had a rack in the parlor where they would bring
> out some bacon and hang it to show it off. That was a sign of
> wealth and that a man "could really bring home the bacon."

Like *dirt poor*, the authors of *Life in the 1500s* have included another twentieth-century Americanism in the piece. The phrase
to bring home the bacon only dates to 1909, first used by cartoonist Thomas Aloysius "T. A. D." Dorgan. (Yes, the cartoonist of
the hot dog legend can legitimately be credited with this one.)
"He'll bring home the bacon as sure as you're wearing a hat."[7]

The phrase was probably never intended to be a literal description of bringing home meat for the table; rather it is simply an alliterative metaphor for success and ability to provide
for one's family.

Chew the Fat

> They would cut off a little [bacon] to share with guests and
> they would all sit around and "chew the fat."

The authors of the e-mail hoax score a bit better with this one.
At least it is not a twentieth-century phrase. Instead, it is from
the nineteenth. The phrase dates to 1885. It originally meant to
grumble or complain. The sense of idle conversation and
telling tall tales is an American usage dating to 1907.[8]

Trencher / Trench Mouth

> Most people didn't have pewter plates though, they all had
> trenchers, that was a piece of wood with the middle scooped

out like a bowl. They never washed their boards and a lot of times worms would get into the wood. After eating off the trencher with worms they would get "trench mouth."

A *trencher* is pretty much as it is described in the e-mail message. It is simply another word for a plate, although it was common in the sixteenth century to have metal or pewter trenchers as well as wooden ones. And often, trenchers were made out of bread, which would be eaten after the food on top had been consumed. The word crossed the English Channel with the Normans and is ultimately from the Old French *tranchouoir*, a verb meaning to cut. *Trenchers* were originally cutting boards and over time the meaning of the word evolved to mean a plate.[9] Trenchers of whatever type, however, were washed after meals.

The term *trench mouth*, however, has nothing to do with Elizabethan England. It is the common name for necrotizing ulcerative gingivitus and the term dates to World War I. Conditions in the trenches of the Western Front led to bacterial infections, like *trench mouth*. It is caused by bacteria, not by worms. While the disease was certainly around in the sixteenth century, this name for it was not. It was the trenches of 1914-18 war that gave it this name.[10]

Bed and Board

If you were going traveling and wanted to stay at an Inn they usually provided the bed but not the board.

While they do not explicitly state it, the authors of *Life in the 1500s* clearly imply that the word *board*, meaning food, stems from the practice of using wooden trenchers. This is simply not correct.

Instead, the word *board* is a reference to a table where food is served. The use of board to refer to a meal table dates to ca. 1200. The transfer of meaning to the food itself dates to the Middle English period, not Elizabethan England. This sense was used by Chaucer in his *Canterbury Tales* ca. 1386. The following is from his *Canon Yeoman's Tale*: "That she wolde suffre hym no thyng for to paye/ For bord ne clothyng, wente he never so gaye."[11]

Upper Crust

> The workers would get the burnt bottom of the loaf, the
> family would get the middle and guests would get the top,
> or the "upper crust".

As with trencher, the author scores partial points for this one. Providing the upper crust of a loaf of bread to a social superior or guest was considered good manners during the period. John Russell in his ca. 1460 *The boke of nurture, folowyng Englondis gise* writes: "kutt þe (the) vpper crust for youre souerayne (sovereign)."

But here Russell is using the term literally, to mean a crust of bread, not as a symbol for high society. This courtesy is not the source of the modern term *upper crust* that denotes aristocracy.

This modern sense of the *upper crust* only dates to the nineteenth century. It comes from a general metaphor of the upper crust of anything being at the peak, not from any specific custom of table manners.[12]

Wake

> They also had lead cups and when they would drink their
> ale or whiskey. [*sic*] The combination would sometimes

knock them out for a couple of days. [. . .] Also, maybe not all of the people they were burying were dead. So they would lay them out on the kitchen table for a couple of days, the family would gather around and eat and drink and wait and see if they would wake up. That's where the custom of holding a "wake" came from.

The hoaxers get a few word origins partially right and one begins to have hope for the rest of the piece. Then they come out with an absurdity like their explanation for the word *wake*. Let us ignore the fact that alcohol drunk out of a lead drinking cup will not induce coma. (Well, maybe it will if one drinks enough to induce alcohol poisoning, but lead poisoning rarely causes comas in adults.) The practice of holding a *wake*, or vigil, over the dead has nothing to do with waiting to see if the dead would wake up. Although burial alive sometimes did happen and many were afraid of its happening (even though it was very rare, nowhere near the one in twenty-five figure given in the e-mail), it is not the origin of a *wake*. The *wake* was originally a prayer vigil where family and friends would pray for the soul of the deceased.

The word is from the Old English *wacu* and is related to the modern word *watch*. Its use to denote a funeral vigil dates to ca. 1412. Its use to denote other types of prayer vigils, notably the vigil conducted on the eve of knighthood, is older. Over time, the term came to be associated with the social interactions accompanying a funeral and lost the association with a prayer vigil.[13]

Graveyard Shift

One out of 25 coffins were that way and they realized they had still been burying people alive. So they thought they

would tie a string on their wrist and lead it through the coffin
and up through the ground and tie it to a bell. Someone
would have to sit out in the graveyard all night to listen for
the bell. That is how the saying "graveyard shift" was made.

Graveyard shift, a term for a late-night work shift, dates to the
turn of the twentieth century. The nautical term *graveyard
watch* appears in 1895. The year 1907 sees the move to land-
based industry and the word *shift* added in place of *watch*.
Both versions are American in origin and have nothing to do
with Elizabethan England.[14]

Nor does the term have anything to do with men stationed
in graveyards listening for those accidentally buried alive (and
neither is it a reference to standing watch to prevent medical
students from robbing graves in search of cadavers as is sometimes claimed in other versions). Instead, the term simply
evokes the desolation and loneliness of late-night work.

Saved by the Bell and Dead Ringer

If the bell would ring they would know that someone was
"saved by the bell" or he was a "dead ringer".

Again, this one is not even close. The phrase *saved by the bell* is
boxing slang. The phrase is first attested to in a dictionary of
boxing terms in 1954, although since this citation is a dictionary,
the term is certainly somewhat older in actual use. There is a
reference to the bell saving a boxer that appears in the November 1932 issue of *Ring* magazine, but it does not use the familiar
phrasing: "Floored in the first session by a terrific right to the
jaw, the bell saving the Jersey boy at the count of seven."[15]

Like *saved by the bell*, the term *dead ringer* has nothing to do with life in Elizabethan England or, for that matter, with death. Instead, *ringer* has its origin in late-nineteenth-century horseracing, meaning a horse that passes for another in a race. The term appears in 1890. From horseracing, the term spread to other, more legitimate activities. The term *dead ringer* appears as U.S. slang in 1891. The *dead* actually has nothing to do with death, but rather refers to precision, as in *dead on, dead center*, and *dead heat*.

The term probably has origins going back to the beginning of the eighteenth century when the verb *to ring* was first used to denote the testing of a coin to see if it was counterfeit. People would literally strike a coin with the finger or another object to see if it rang. If it did, it was genuine.

While there is no evidence of an intermediate use of *ringer* to mean a counterfeit coin that could pass as genuine, it seems likely that the counterfeiting term is the source of the horseracing term. (It is not surprising that there would be gaps in our knowledge of underworld slang; it is not like counterfeiters published books on how they conducted their trade.)[16]

So in the end, what are we to make of the *Life in the 1500s* e-mail? While it contains some linguistic half-truths, we must conclude that it is mostly bunk, a hoax. And while it may be the most common linguistic e-mail hoax, it is not the only one out there. There are many others, including one that ascribes a false acronymic origin to the word *shit*. This and other false acronymic origins are the subject of the next chapter.

Posh,
Phat Pommies

*A*nother bit of etymological e-mail lore is the *Ship High in
Transit* explanation for the origin of the word *shit*. It began making the internet rounds in August 2002, positing an
acronymic origin for the word:

> Ever wonder where the word "shit" comes from. Well here it
> is. Certain types of manure used to be transported (as every-
> thing was back then) by ship. In dry form it weighed a lot
> less, but once water (at sea) hit it, it not only became heav-
> ier, but the process of fermentation began again, which by-
> product is methane gas. As the stuff was stored below decks
> in bundles you can see what could (and did) happen.
> Methane began to build up below decks and the first time
> someone came below at night with a lantern—BOOOOM!

Several ships were destroyed in this manner before it was discovered what was happening. After that, the bundles of manure were always stamped with the term "S.H.I.T" on them which meant to the sailors to "Ship High In Transit" or in other words, high enough off the lower decks so that any water that came into the hold would not touch this volatile cargo and start the production of methane.

Bet you didn't know that one.[2]

This is a variant of a somewhat older tale that appeared in the Usenet newsgroup rec.humor in May 1999. This earlier version is a bit confusing as it does not explain why the manure should be "shipped high":

In the 1800's, cow pie's [*sic*] were collected on the prarie [*sic*] and boxed and loaded on steam ships to burn instead of wood. Wood was not only hard to find, but heavy to move around and store.

When the boxes of cow pie's [*sic*] were in the sun for days on board the ships, they would smell bad. So when the manure was boxed up, they stamped the outside of the box, S.H.I.T. . . . which means Ship High In Transit.

When people came aboard the ship and said, "Oh what is that smell!" They were told it was shit.

That is where the saying came from. . . . It smells like shit![3]

And this joke is not even the origin of the tale. A January 30, 1999, post to the newsgroup rec.aviation.rotorcraft turns up the following claim:

And for your information, S.H.I.T. originated from the English cargo ships, where it was on the crates, that should be: Ship High In Transit[4]

So the story had some life before it wormed its way onto the internet.

This alleged acronymic origin is not even close to the truth. *Shit* is a very old word, with an Old English root. It is first recorded as a verb, *to shite*, in the beginning of the fourteenth century. The noun is from the late sixteenth century. While *shit* does not appear until the Middle English period, etymologists have determined that it has a probable root in an Old English word, **scítan*. (In standard etymological notation the asterisk means that the root is assumed to have existed, but has not actually been found in extant texts.) It has cognates in most of the other Germanic languages and shares a common root with modern equivalents like the German *scheissen*. Its use as an interjection is of quite recent vintage, not found until the 1920s.[5]

The *Ship High in Transit* tale illustrates one of the most common forms of etymological urban legend, the acronymic word origin. As H. L. Mencken notes in the quote that begins this chapter, people have an endless fascination with acronyms. Acronyms can be fun. Most of us, at some time or other, have probably sat around with friends and made up humorous acronyms. It is only a short hop from creating acronyms to believing that various words are created from acronyms.

As a result, there are mythical acronymic origins for any number of words such as those in the title of this chapter: *posh* (port out, starboard home), *phat* (pretty hips and thighs), and *Pommy* (prisoner of mother England).

The fact is, however, that very few words actually begin their life as acronyms, and most of these are proper nouns like *NATO* (North Atlantic Treaty Organization) and *NORAD* (North American Air Defense Command). Also, forming words from acronyms is a distinctly twentieth- (and now twenty-first-) century phenomenon. There is only one known pre-twentieth-century word with an acronymic origin and it was in vogue for only a short time in 1886. The word is *colinderies* or *colinda*, an acronym for the Colonial and Indian Exposition held in London in that year.[6]

The next words with acronymic origins are a pair of trade names. *Nabisco*, an acronym for the National Biscuit Company, was registered as a trademark in 1901.[7] The second is *Seroco*, an acronym for Sears, Roebuck and Company that was used to market a variety of products in the early days of the twentieth century. The name *Seroco* is first known to have appeared in a classified ad in 1902, but it is probably several years older than that.[8] The next known acronym is the World War I term *ANZAC*, meaning Australian–New Zealand Army Corps, from 1915.[9] The term *acronym* itself only dates from the 1940s, from the Greek *akros*, meaning point, and *onuma*, meaning name.[10]

At this point, we should get the definitions of a few terms straight. An *acronym* is a word formed from the initial letter or letters of each word in a phrase. An acronym is pronounceable as a word, like NATO. An *initialism* is an abbreviation formed from the initial letter or letters of each word in a phrase, but is not pronounceable as a single word, e.g., BBC, British Broadcasting Company. A *backronym* is an acronym formed on an existing word, e.g., START for Strategic Arms Reduction Treaty. Some expand the meaning of the word *acronym* to include initialisms and backronyms, but I will preserve the distinction here to maintain clarity.

Although only one pre-twentieth-century example of an acronym exists, *colinderies* or *colinda*, the backronym, while rare, was known in earlier times.

Ichthys

An early example of a backronym, although not an English one, is the Greek word *ichthys*, meaning fish. Early Christians used the word to stand for *Iesous Christos Theou Huios Soter* (Jesus Christ, Son of God, Savior). Fish were associated with Christ as the fisher of men, and the fish symbol was a common hieroglyph used by the early church to denote Christ and Christians (and it is still found on the bumpers and tailgates of many modern automobiles). *Ichthys*, which dates as far back as Homer in the eighth century B.C., is one of several Greek words for fish. The use of *ichthys* as an acronym by the early Christian church appears as early as the second century A.D., but may have even earlier roots.[11]

Cabal

A later English example of a backronym is *cabal*. The word entered the English language from the French *cabale* and ultimately comes from the Hebrew *cabala*, the medieval body of arcane and mystical Jewish teachings. The earliest use of the word in English is in 1616, in the original, Hebrew sense. By 1637 the word was being used in the sense of a secret, and in the sense of a group of conspirators by 1646.[12]

The backronym *cabal* was formed from the names of five ministers of King Charles II. The ministers, Clifford, Arlington,

Buckingham, Ashley, and Lauderdale, were at the bottom of various political intrigues in the early 1670s. According to history, these five, plus others, defaulted on the national debt by closing the exchequer in 1670, started a war with Holland in 1672, and entered into an alliance with the hated French in 1673. The English use of the word *cabal* to mean a group of conspirators predates the nefarious schemes of these five by at least twenty-five years.

Initialisms, as opposed to acronyms, existed in the nineteenth century, but they were not common until the twentieth: examples include I.L.P. for Independent Labour Party and I.D.B. for Illicit Diamond Buyer. A smattering of acronyms and initialisms appear in the opening decades of the twentieth century. In the 1920s, the growth in initialisms and acronyms accelerates and in the 30s and 40s there is an explosion in their usage coinciding with the New Deal and World War II. The two most famous acronyms did not appear until the 1940s and 50s. *Radar*, or Radio Detection and Ranging, debuts in 1941. *Scuba*, or Self-Contained Underwater Breathing Apparatus, makes its appearance in 1952.[13]

Any claims for a pre-twentieth-century acronym must be viewed with great suspicion. Such a thing is not inconceivable, especially if it allegedly dates to the second half of the nineteenth century, but it is unlikely. There is one other acronym that is often claimed to be from the nineteenth century that could be so. But to date no record of its use from that century has been found.

AWOL

The acronym in question is the word *AWOL*, or *Absent With Out Leave*. Popular myth would have the term dating to the

American Civil War in the 1860s. In their otherwise excellent 1997 book *America in So Many Words*, linguists David Barnhart and Allan Metcalf repeat the Civil War claim, lending the story respectability. Barnhart and Metcalf rely on H. L. Mencken's *The American Language* as a source for this claim.[14] Mencken himself does not plump for a Civil War origin. Instead he correctly dates the acronym to the World War I period, but he does include the following quotation from a 1944 Civil War history in a footnote:

> [In the Confederate Army] unwarranted absences of short duration were often unpunished and in many other cases offenders received such trivial sentences as reprimand by a company officer, digging a stump, carrying a rail for an hour or two, wearing a placard inscribed with the letters AWOL. . . .[15]

Despite the appearance of the tale in history books, there is no evidence that the abbreviation *AWOL* was in use during the American Civil War. There are various claims of photographs purporting to show this punishment, but to date no one has actually been able to produce these photographs or any other documentation of an 1860s use of the acronym. All we have are claims made some eighty years (or later) after the fact.

One reason the Civil War tale is so suspicious is its marked similarity to two other linguistic urban legends, the origins of *fuck* and *For Unlawful Carnal Knowledge*, and *wogs* and *Working on Government Service* (cf. *fuck* and *wog* later in this chapter, pp. 87, 95). Both these tales have prisoners or workers wearing shirts bearing initialisms. Both are false. We have seen how urban legends change details, spawning different variants of the same basic story. Such may be the case here, with the fixed element being prisoners forced to wear a sign bearing an abbreviation of their crime and the variable element being the acronym in question. This folk belief may have its ultimate origin in Nathaniel Hawthorne's *The Scarlet Letter* (1850), in which protagonist Hester Prynne is forced to wear a scarlet letter on her breast signifying her crime, presumably an "A" for adultery.

Another factor in the popularity of the *AWOL* tale is the fact that the Civil War is a topic much loved by hobbyists and amateur historians. Any topic that excites the passions of hobbyists and fans tends to generate false etymologies (see chapter 4, p. 103: CANOE).

While unlikely, an 1860s origin for *AWOL* is not utterly implausible. After all, the term does have its origins in the American military, and it is not too much of a stretch to extend its life back another half century. Furthermore, the phrase *absent without leave* does in fact date to the Civil War, even if its abbreviation does not. Civil War general Benjamin Butler writes in 1861: "At 'Camp Chase,' all the members of the company being present (saving those absent without leave), by written ballots in my presence the members of the company of twenty one (21) years and upwards selected their officers by election."[16]

There are numerous citations of the phrase *absent without leave* in Civil War-era documents, but none of *AWOL*. Someone may yet produce proof that the abbreviation is indeed of Civil War vintage. But until that happens, a Civil War origin must be discounted.

So if it does not date to the Civil War, how old is *AWOL*? It is reliably dated to American participation in World War I, 1917-18. This would put it among the first acronyms, but still not older than *ANZAC*. Was it pronounced as a single word, making it a true acronym, or as individual letters, making it an initialism? There is evidence to indicate that it was pronounced as a single word as early as 1919. In *AWOL—All Wrong Old Laddiebuck*, an animated film by Charles Bowers, a woman presents her calling card to a soldier and it reads "Miss Awol." She then lures him away from camp without permission. The film is silent of course, given the 1919 date, but the calling card indicates that *AWOL* is pronounced as a word, making it a true acronym and not just an initialism.[17]

The evidence is clear. Any claim of pre-twentieth-century acronymic word origins must be viewed with great suspicion. Still, this does not deter people from continuing to associate false acronymic etymologies with some very old words, much older than *AWOL*. Perhaps the most popular acronymic myth is that surrounding the origin of most infamous four-letter word.

Fuck

Popular etymologies agree, unfortunately incorrectly, that *fuck* is an acronym meaning either *Fornication under Consent of the King* or *For Unlawful Carnal Knowledge*. These tales tell of how people required special permission in order to procreate or how medieval prisoners, guilty of adultery or other sex crimes, were forced to wear this word on their clothing.

Tracing the etymology of *fuck* is difficult, as it has been under a taboo for most of its existence and early citations of the word are rare. The earliest known use is from ca. 1475 in a poem written in a mix of Latin and English and entitled *Flen flyys*. The relevant lines read: "Non sunt in celi/ quia fuccant uuiuys of heli." Translated, it reads: "They [the monks] are not in heaven/ because they fuck the wives of Ely [a town near Cambridge]." *Fuccant* is a pseudo-Latin word and in the original manuscript it is written in cipher to further disguise it.[18]

Some sources cite an alleged appearance of the word in 1278 as a personal name, *John le Fucker*. The problem with this is that no one has properly identified the document this name supposedly appears in, and it may not truly be a thirteenth-century citation. This alleged 1278 name can only be traced to 1949, when it was mentioned in Carl Buck's dictionary of Indo-European roots. Unfortunately, Buck never identifies the source so we cannot check its validity or the context in which the name appears.[19] The belief that this thirteenth-century name is the origin of the word *fuck* got a boost in 1990 when John Ayto uncritically repeated Buck's claim in his *Dictionary of Word Origins*.[20] Buck's dictionary is a rather arcane source, not very familiar to the public. Ayto's, however, is geared for the general reader and is widely cited.

If this name is real and does indeed date to 1278, there is still no guarantee that this is an instance of the word *fuck*. Instead, the name is more likely a variant of the surname *Fulcher* (soldier). Other thirteenth-century spellings of that or similar names include *Fuker, Foucher, Fucher, Foker*, and *Foucar*. It is almost certain that this is just another spelling of that name.[21]

Such is the nature of taboo words; they defy the best efforts to find their roots since, because they are taboo, no one writes them down. Without written citations, tracing the origin of a word is impossible.

Shakespeare is a source for the origins of many words, but he does not use this one, although he does hint at it from time to time for comic effect, letting us know the word was well known in Elizabethan times. In *Merry Wives of Windsor* (IV.i) he gives us the pun *focative case*. In *Henry V* (IV.iv), the character Pistol threatens to *firk* a French soldier, a word meaning to strike, but commonly used as an Elizabethan euphemism for *fuck*. In the same play (III.iv), Princess Katherine confuses the English words *foot* and *gown* for the French *foutre* and *coun* (fuck and cunt, respectively) with comic results. Other poets and writers do use the word, although its appearances are rare. Robert Burns, for example, uses it in an unpublished manuscript.

The taboo was so strong that for 170 years, from 1795 to 1965, *fuck* did not appear in a single general dictionary of the English language. As late as 1948, the publishers of *The Naked and the Dead* persuaded Norman Mailer to use the euphemism *fug* instead, resulting in Dorothy Parker's alleged comment upon meeting Mailer: "So you're the man who can't spell fuck." [22] *Fuck* does not begin to appear with any frequency in published sources until the 1960s.

The root is undoubtedly Germanic, as it has cognates in other Northern European languages: Middle Dutch *fokken* meaning to thrust, to copulate with; dialectal Norwegian *fukka* meaning to copulate; and dialectal Swedish *focka* meaning to strike, push, copulate, and *fock* meaning penis. Both French and Italian have similar words, *foutre* and *fottere*, respectively. These derive from the Latin *futuere*.

While these cognates exist, they are not the source of *fuck*. Rather, all these words probably come from a common root. Most of the early known usages of the English word come from Scotland, leading some scholars to believe that the word comes from Scandinavian sources, because the Viking influence on English was stronger in Scotland and the north of England. Others disagree, believing that the number of northern citations reflects that the taboo was weaker in Scotland and the north, resulting in more surviving usages. The fact that there are citations from the same period, albeit fewer of them, from southern England seems to bear out this latter theory.

Before we depart from the discussion of this word, we have to touch upon another popular legend about its origin. During the Hundred Years' War the French would cut the middle finger off the hands of captured English archers so that they could no longer draw the strings of their deadly yew longbows. Because of this, English archers would taunt the French by raising their middle fingers and exclaiming that they could still "pluck yew," hence the four-letter word.

Now this is obviously a joke, a pun. It is doubtful that whoever came up with this howler meant for it to be taken seriously. But this joke has gained urban legend status thanks to the internet. Its canonical version began appearing on the internet in December 1996:

> The "Car Talk" show (on NPR) with Click and Clack, the Tappet Brothers, have a feature called the "Puzzler." Their most recent "Puzzler" was about the Battle of Agincourt. The French, who were overwhelmingly favored to win the battle, threatened to cut a certain body part off of all captured English soldiers so that they could never fight again. The English won in a major upset and waved the body part in question at the French in defiance. The puzzler was: What was this body part? This is the answer submitted by a listener:
>
> Dear Click and Clack,
>
> Thank you for the Agincourt "Puzzler," which clears up some profound questions of etymology, folklore and emotional symbolism. The body part which the French proposed to cut off of the English after defeating them was, of course, the middle finger, without which it is impossible to draw the renowned English longbow. This famous weapon was made of the native English yew tree, and so the act of drawing the longbow was known as "plucking yew". Thus, when the victorious English waved their middle fingers at

the defeated French, they said, "See, we can still pluck yew! PLUCK YEW!"

Over the years some "folk etymologies" have grown up around this symbolic gesture. Since "pluck yew" is rather difficult to say (like "pleasant mother pheasant plucker", which is who you had to go to for the feathers used on the arrows), the difficult consonant cluster at the beginning has gradually changed to a labiodental fricative "f", and thus the words often used in conjunction with the one-finger-salute are mistakenly thought to have something to do with an intimate encounter. It is also because of the pheasant feathers on the arrows that the symbolic gesture is known as "giving the bird."[23]

But this version does not accurately reflect what was said on the National Public Radio program *Car Talk*. Each week on that program, the hosts, Tom and Ray Magliozzi, present a "puzzler," a riddle or puzzle that is often humorous. The puzzler in question, which was asked on March 21, 1996, and the answer given the next week on March 28, made no mention of "plucking yew" and was not even about the middle-finger gesture. Instead the gesture in question was about the "V for Victory" sign, and the story had the French cutting off both the index and middle fingers of English archers they had captured. The Magliozzis did make mention that some believed that it was just one finger that was cut off and that another gesture might have had its origin at Agincourt, but that is as far as they went.[24] The letter given in the canonical version may have been sent to the Magliozzis, but it was not read on the air. Sometime between the show's airing in March and the appearance of the letter on the internet in December the story had changed, and the "pluck yew" aspect was added.

Such is the nature of urban legends; the details are highly malleable as long as they are part of oral tradition. But once the legend is transmitted in written form, whether via fax, photocopy, or internet, it becomes stable and changes are harder to introduce.

News and Tips

Four-letter words like *shit* and *fuck* are not the only terms to be accorded acronymic origins in popular folklore. Sometimes everyday, innocuous words are falsely accorded this distinction. Such is the case with *news* and *tip*, two words commonly said to arise from acronyms.

News, according to the myth, is an acronym for the cardinal points on a compass: north, east, west, and south. How this particular myth arose is a bit of a mystery. After all, the true origin is patently obvious. *News* refers to tidings about new things or events. The modern sense of tidings or information about recent events dates to 1423, although the word did not enter common use until after 1500. It is from the Old French *noveles* and ultimately from the Latin *nova*.[25]

The myth may have begun life as a classroom mnemonic device for remembering the points of the compass and students conflated the mnemonic with the origin of the word. Although, the value of the mnemonic device is somewhat suspect because news does not present the directions in order. That would be *nesw* or *nwse*.

Similarly, the word *tip*, meaning a gratuity given to a waiter or servant, is often thought to be an acronym for *to insure promptness*. *Tip* began life as an underworld cant term meaning to pass on, to hand to, and especially to pass on a small sum of money. It may be an offshoot of the sense of *tip* meaning to hit or tap lightly, but this is by no means certain. The sense meaning to pass on a sum of money dates to at least 1610. The modern sense of passing a sum intended as a gratuity to a servant appears about a century later. The noun dates to at least 1755.[26]

Golf

The Augusta National Golf Club, which hosts the Masters Tournament each year, may not permit women to join (at least they do not as I am writing this in 2003), but despite this the term *golf* is not from an acronym standing for *Gentlemen Only, Ladies Forbidden*. Like all pre-twentieth-century terms, this acronymic origin is false. The exact origin of the game's name, however, is uncertain. The game of golf is first mentioned in a 1457 act of the Scottish Parliament when King James II of Scotland attempted to ban the game because soldiers were spending too much time playing instead of training: "And at þe fut bal ande þe golf be vtterly cryt downe and nocht vsyt." (And at the football and the golf be utterly cried down and not used.) It is a sentiment many "golf widows" of today undoubtedly share.

While the origin of the name *golf* is unknown, there is some reasoned speculation as to where it comes from. Often, the Dutch word *kolf* is suggested as a possible origin. The word is used in Dutch to refer to clubs or bats used in a variety of sports. One problem is that the Dutch word is not used for the name of any sport, only various pieces of equipment. Also, the K or hard C sounds do not appear in the early Scottish uses of the term, which all begin with a G sound. Finally, the Dutch word does not appear until after 1457. Modern Scots dialect has the word *gowf*, meaning a blow or a strike or to strike. This may be related, but it could just as easily come from the name of the game.[27]

There is another origin story for *golf* that is worth mentioning. It has never achieved the status of urban legend, probably because it is so obviously fictional, but it is repeated quite often and the originator was a leading linguistic scholar. The story is found in J.R.R. Tolkien's book *The Hobbit*: "[Bullroarer Took] charged the ranks of the goblins of Mount Gram in the Battle of the Green Fields, and knocked their king Golfimbul's head clean off with a wooden club. It sailed a hundred yards through the air and went down a rabbit hole, and in this way the battle was won and the game of golf invented at the same moment."[28]

While Tolkien is best remembered for writing the famed fantasy books, he was professor of linguistics at Oxford and was one of the world's leading experts on Old English. Here he is just having a bit of fun with alleged etymologies.

Spud

Sometimes, however, linguists create or repeat a spurious etymology that generates or reinforces a linguistic urban legend. We saw an example of this with *AWOL*. Another example is in Mario Pei's 1949 book *The Story of Language*: "The potato, for its part, was in disrepute some centuries ago. Some Englishmen who did not fancy potatoes formed a 'Society for the Prevention of Unwholesome Diet.' The initials of the main words in this title gave rise to 'spud.' "[29]

This etymology is wrong. *Spud* actually comes from the digging implement used to uproot potatoes. *Spud* originally (ca. 1440) was a term for a short knife or dagger. It subsequently was used to denote a variety of digging tools, some used for potatoes. Around 1845 the word transferred over to the tuber itself. Why knives were once called *spuds* is unknown, but the origin is not an acronym.[30]

Pei eventually corrected this error. In his 1965 revision, he wrote: "The potato, for its part, was in disrepute some centuries ago. Some Englishmen who did not fancy potatoes formed a 'Society for the Prevention of Unwholesome Diet,' but the people of England kept right on eating potatoes."[31]

But the damage was done. Many of his readers took the acronymic origin as genuine. And many of those reading the 1965 version continued to read an acronymic origin into his words. Pei never explicitly denied the acronymic origin. Even today, more than fifty years after Pei wrote the book, readers of my website refer to Pei as an authority for the acronymic origin for *spud*. However, his is not the only alleged acronym, as *spud* is also sometimes claimed to stand for *Stop Poisoning Ulster's Diets*.

Wog

Earlier, we mentioned *wogs* and the false belief that it stems from an acronym for *Working on Government Service*. Allegedly, workers on the Suez Canal wore the letters W.O.G.S. on their shirts—a fanciful, but untrue tale. Nor is this the only alleged acronym for the word. Other acronymic phrases include

- Westernized Oriental Gentleman
- Worthy Oriental Gentleman
- Wily Oriental Gentleman
- Wonderful Oriental Gentleman

Wog is chiefly a British term, a holdover from the days of the empire. It is a disparaging term for an Indian (from India, not America), an Arab, or any other Asian. More recently, *wog* has been used to refer to any foreigner, with jokes like "the wogs begin at Calais," or even to anyone outside the greater London area.

While the origin of *wog* is not known with absolute certainty, most etymologists agree that it is likely a clipping of *golliwog*, a black-faced doll with frizzy hair. *Golliwog* was coined by Bertha Upton in a popular children's book published in 1895, *The Adventures of Two Dutch Dolls and a Golliwogg*. By 1907, *golliwog* was in generic use for anything Asian.

Nylon

Another invented term that is frequently given an acronymic etymology in popular myth is *nylon*. In this case, it is easy to see why someone might think it was an acronym. The word is distinctly twentieth century, and it has no intrinsic meaning. Two acronyms are often cited: The first is New York and London, allegedly because the fiber was produced by collaboration of research labs in those two cities or because DuPont launched the product simultaneously in those two cities. While *nylon* was indeed introduced to the public in New York, London had nothing to do with either the product development or launch. The second acronym is a bit more sinister: *Now You've Lost, Old Nippon*, supposedly a reference to DuPont's belief that their product would destroy the Japanese silk market.

The revolutionary fiber, created by DuPont chemist Wallace Carothers in 1935, was introduced to the public at the New York World's Fair in 1938. The name is a creation of DuPont's marketing department. DuPont went through a lengthy selection process before settling on *nylon*. One of the choices considered by DuPont was an acronym, *Duparooh*, standing for *DuPont Pulls a Rabbit Out of a Hat*, but this was rejected as too silly.[32]

One suggestion that almost made it was *No-run*, from the alleged feature that nylon stockings would not run. But since this is not the case and nylon stockings do in fact run, the name was rejected. But *no-run* may have been the basis from which the DuPont marketing team worked to create the name *nylon*.[33] The *–on* suffix was probably chosen to evoke *cotton* and *rayon*. Like many trade names, *nylon* was ultimately chosen precisely because it did not mean anything, making it easier to defend against trademark infringement.[34]

SOS

Another term that was deliberately coined without a meaning is the international Morse code distress signal, *SOS*. And it is also another word with multiple false acronymic origins. *SOS* does not stand for any of the following:

- Save Our Souls
- Save Our Ship
- Stop Other Signals
- Sure of Sinking

SOS was chosen as the universal distress signal by the International Radio Telegraph Convention of July 1908 because the combination of three dots followed by three dashes followed by three dots (. . . – – – . . .) was easy to send and easy to recognize. Another choice feature is that the single nine-character signal stands out against the background chatter of three-character Morse code letters. The letters themselves are meaningless.[35]

The first recorded mention of a false acronymic origin is in association with the *Titanic* sinking of 1912. The *Titanic* was the first ship that actually used the new signal. This was widely reported in the press and the association with the famed ship probably accounts for the endurance of the false acronym story.

Prior to 1908, the high seas distress signal consisted of the letters *CQD*, which many took to mean *Come Quickly, Danger*. Like *SOS*, this older term is also meaningless. It is a combination of the letters *CQ*—the standard radio hail meaning "calling all stations" or "is anyone out there?"—and the nonsense letter *D*. Some suppose that the *CQ* stands for *seek you* and that the *D* stands for *distress*, but this is not documented. Use of *CQD* continued past 1908 and the *Titanic's* initial distress calls used this older signal. It was not until the ship was near sinking that the radiomen sent out the new *SOS* signal.

Pommy

OK, so what about the chapter title? What about *Posh, Phat Pommies?* What is their significance? Actually, they have no significance beyond alliteration and sharing false acronymic origin legends.

Most Americans probably are not familiar with the word *Pommy*. It is a derogatory Australian slang term for an Englishman. It is often found in the form *Pommy bastard*. The acronymic origin refers back to the old days when Australia was still a British penal colony. Allegedly, new prisoners were referred to with the initials *P.O.M.E.*, for *Prisoner of Mother England*. Some versions of the story have the convicts wearing the initials on their shirts, as in *fuck* or *wog*. Others claim that these letters were carved in the walls of the Port Arthur jail in Tasmania. No evidence has been produced to substantiate these claims.

There is no record of the phrase *Prisoner of Mother England* ever being used to refer to British convicts. Further, the transportation of convicts to Australia ended in 1868, but the term *Pommy* does not appear until 1915. The clipped form *pom* appears a few years later in 1919.[36] Of course, it is possible that the acronym was created after the penal colonies were closed in an attempt to evoke Australia's history.

So, where did the term come from if not an acronym? The origin is not known for certain. The most common suggestion is that it is a clipping of *pomegranate*, which is rhyming slang for *immigrant*. The rhyming slang is reinforced by the fact that newcomers from Britain would quickly have their faces burned red in the Australian sun, like a pomegranate. This is a plausible origin, although there is no real evidence to support it.

Phat

The hip-hop slang term *phat* is frequently given an acronymic origin as well. The term refers to something desirable, especially something that is sexually desirable, like a pretty woman. The exact acronym varies with the telling, often depending on how explicit one wants to get:

- Pretty Hot and Tempting
- Pretty Hips and Thighs
- Pussy Hips Ass and Tits

However, there is no evidence supporting any of these origins.

Instead, *phat* is simply a slang respelling of *fat*. Such respellings are common in slang (e.g., *phreak* for *freak*). And *fat* has a long history of meaning rich, abundant, or desirable—in English since the sixteenth century, and in other languages for far longer. *Phat* has been a staple of African-American slang since at least 1963.[37] The specific sexual connotation of it is likely just a specialization of the general meaning.

Posh

If something is *phat*, then there is a good chance it is also pretty *posh*. This is another word with an apocryphal acronymic origin. The myth has it that *posh* is an acronym for *Port Out, Starboard Home*. Supposedly, this acronym was printed on first-class tickets issued by the Peninsular and Oriental Steam Navigation Company going from England to India and back. The port side on the outward leg of the journey would have the coolest cabins (or alternatively the cabins with the best view). The same would be true of the starboard cabins on the return trip. Thus, *posh* came to mean swank, elegant, or fashionable. Unfortunately for this excellent story, no tickets with *Posh* stamped on them have been found and company records reveal no sign of the phrase.

The earliest unambiguous use of *posh* to mean high class is from the September 25, 1918, issue of the British humor magazine *Punch*: "Oh, yes, Mater, we had a posh time of it down there."

There is a possible use of the term some fifteen years earlier. In 1903, P. G. Wodehouse in his *Tales of St. Austin's* wrote: "That waistcoat . . . being quite the most push thing of the sort in Cambridge." Whether this was a printer's error or Wodehouse actually meant to use *push* is not known (several later editors "corrected" this to read *posh*).

But there are even older uses of the word in different senses that tell the tale of its development. *Posh* dates back to at least 1867 when used to mean a dandy or a fop. The best guess as to its origin is that it derives from Romany, the language of the

Rom (commonly known as Gypsies). In Romany, *posh* means half and is used in monetary terms like *posh-houri*, or half-pence, and *posh-kooroona*, meaning half-crown. The progression runs from money to a fancy dresser to high class.[38]

In contrast, the earliest claim to the acronymic origin only dates to October 17, 1935, in the *London Times Literary Supplement*, in which it is claimed to be of American origin. The earliest association with the P&O steam line comes two years later, and almost twenty after the still current sense of the word was established.[39]

As we shall see in the next chapter, *posh* is not the only term given a false nautical origin; despite the many correct accounts of nautical word origins, false tales of this sort abound. Any field with enthusiasts will generate such fictions and sailing and the sea are no exception.

Canoe

One of the common patterns in linguistic legendry is for people to attribute the origins of words and catch phrases to a field that interests them. Now, there are many English words and phrases that do indeed come from the sea. After all, Brittania ruled the seas for centuries and America has also maintained a rich maritime tradition. It is only natural that things nautical would contribute to our vocabulary.

But there is a tendency among some nautical enthusiasts to attribute a maritime origin to just about every word and phrase they can think of. This tendency is so common that one of the participants in the www.wordorigins.org online discussion group dubbed it *CANOE,* or the *Conspiracy to Attribute Nautical Origins to Everything.*

Devil to Pay

Sometimes the beliefs of the canoeists stem from simple confusion over similar words. Such is the case with the phrase *the
devil to pay*. It is commonly asserted that this phrase is nautical
in origin. According to the myth, the *devil* in question is not
Satan, but rather the seam at the ship's keel, the longest on
board. The verb *pay* means to caulk the seam with tar. So *to pay
the devil* is to caulk the seam along the keel of the ship, a long
and arduous task. It is a great explanation, but unfortunately
the evidence does not support it as being the origin of the
phrase. Rather the opposite is true; the phrase probably gave
birth to the nautical term *devil*.

As in other cases, we have to go to the lexicographic record.
The phrase *the devil to pay* first appears in Jonathan Swift's 1711
Journal to Stella, a context that has nothing to do with the sea.
The phrase has at its origin the metaphor of a Faustian bargain.
One pays the devil with one's soul, a very high price.[1]

The devil to pay was indeed used by sailors to mean caulking
the keel's seam, but as a humorous application of the Faustian
metaphor. *Devil* is indeed a word used to refer to the seam
along the keel of a ship, but the term does not appear until
1744, well after the phrase *the devil to pay* was in use. *To pay* is a
nautical verb meaning to smear tar or pitch, dating from 1627.
So it appears as if the sailors used the phrase as a play on their
jargon word *pay*. The nautical use of *devil* probably comes
from the phrase, not vice versa.[2]

Let the Cat out of the Bag

Other supposed nautical phrases are similar to *the devil to pay*
in that they share a similarity with some nautical jargon term.

One such phrase is *let the cat out of the bag*, meaning to disclose a secret.

Until 1881, the Royal Navy used a whip of nine knotted cords, known as the *cat o' nine tails*, as an instrument of punishment on board ship. Often sailors clipped the term to just *the cat*. This name for the whip dates to 1695. *Nine tails* is an obvious reference to the nine knotted cords, but why *cat*? It is probably from a bit of sailor humor: a cat, like a whip, can scratch.³ The bag enters the legend because on board ship the whip was often kept in a sealed bag to protect it from the salt air, keeping it flexible and supple. So, to *let the cat out of the bag* must be to make an admission that results in punishment. Or at least that is what nautical enthusiasts would have.

But this is not the origin of the phrase. Instead, its origin is from landlubbers. The phrase refers to an old scam of selling someone a suckling pig at market and then surreptitiously substituting a cat for the pig. If one lets the cat out of the bag, then the secret is revealed and the fraud discovered. The scam dates to at least 1530, but the phrase does not make its appearance until 1760. Derived from the same scam, there is a similar phrase in French, *vider le sac*, or empty the sack, and another common phrase, *to buy a pig in a poke*.⁴

Another "cat" phrase that is often falsely associated with the nautical cat o' nine tails is *room enough to swing a cat*. Often people, quite understandably, assume that the phrase refers to the space needed to wield a whip. In truth, the phrase predates the appearance of *cat o' nine tails* by at least some thirty years. The phrase is first recorded in 1665 and is a metaphorical reference to swinging a feline by the tail. This early reference calls the phrase a "vulgar saying," indicating that it was well established by that time and not a new coinage.⁵

It is easy to see how one might mistakenly attribute a nautical origin to phrases like *the devil to pay* or *let the cat out of the bag.* The phrases in question bear a similarity to nautical terms and can be reasonably construed to stem from nautical practices. The legends begin as speculation, and as they are repeated again and again among nautical enthusiasts they lose their tentative nature and become statements of "truth." But in other instances the legend is simply made out of whole cloth.

Cold Enough to Freeze the Balls off a Brass Monkey

The tale goes that in the age of sail, cannon balls were kept on ship decks stacked in neat triangles on a brass rack called a monkey. When the temperature dropped, the brass monkey would contract, spilling the cannon balls all over the deck. Hence the phrase *cold enough to freeze the balls off a brass monkey.*

It sounds neat, but the story is not true. First, there is no evidence that the word *monkey* was ever a term used for such a rack or device. No citations of *monkey* being used in such a sense have been presented. Nor did sailing ships stack cannon balls on the decks. Instead, ready shot was kept on wooden planks with holes drilled in them known as *shot racks* or *shot garlands.*[6]

Second, the earliest known use of the phrase is from 1847 in Herman Melville's novel *Omoo*: "To use a hyperbolical phrase of Shorty's, 'It was 'ot enough to melt the nose h'off a brass monkey.'"[7] Note that this version uses *hot* and *melt* as opposed to *cold* and *freeze*, making the idea of metal contracting in the cold less likely as an origin. It is possible that Melville's use of *nose* is a euphemism and the original *balls* is older, but unrecorded. But regardless of which version came first there is no doubt that this early reference is referring to anatomy, not ordnance. The phrase appears to be an Americanism, first appearing in an American work and coming into widespread use among troops in the U.S. Civil War.[8]

Also, there is considerable variation in the phrase. In addition to balls and nose, the *Random House Historical Dictionary of American Slang* records ears, tails, and whiskers being frozen or melted off the hapless brass monkeys. The poor brass monkeys have also had their throats scalded, their pants scared off, and their guts rotted out. The variety of anatomical parts used in the different versions provides further evidence to support an origin in anatomical metaphor.

But there may be some truth to the idea that the expression arose in the navy and could possibly have something to do with cannons. The earliest known citations of use, including Melville's, are in nautical contexts. Also, *monkey* was used in the seventeenth century to denote a type of cannon. A 1650 inventory of ordnance in Edinburgh Castle reads in part: "Short Brasse Munkeys alias Dogs. 10 Iron Munkeys."And James Heath's *Flagellum* of 1672 mentions: "Twenty-eight Brass Drakes called Monkeys." A *drake* is a type of cannon. Furthermore, a *monkey tail* is a nautical term for a handspike used to aim and level a cannon. This term dates to 1822.[9]

Still, there is no proof of linkage between these ordnance uses of *monkey* and the phrase. The seventeenth-century use of *monkey,* meaning a cannon, was obsolete for nearly two centuries before the phrase appears. And while there is a *monkey tail* in the nineteenth-century navy, there is no monkey from which it could freeze off. It seems likely that these ordnance uses of *monkey* and *monkey tail* are unrelated to the phrase.

So how did such a fanciful tale arise? Well, CANOE is certainly partly to blame, but there is another factor at work as well. There is often a desire to euphemize our saltier expressions. Sometimes, this is done like the "freeze the tail off . . ."

examples, with a simple substitution of the offending word. But other times, the expression is kept intact and a non-offensive explanation is created to justify the use of the salty phrase in polite company (cf. *Tinker's Damn* in chapter 6, p. 182). In this case, both factors combined to create a linguistic urban legend.

Over a Barrel

Like let the *cat out of the bag*, the phrase *over a barrel* is often thought to be a reference to punishment in the Royal Navy. A sailor, sentenced to flogging, was forced to bend over a barrel and was then whipped. Someone who had been caught in a crime would literally be placed *over a barrel*, or so the legend would have it.

While barrels may have occasionally been used for this purpose in the navy, it was not usual practice. Instead, a sailor was tied to a wooden grate for flogging. If the punishment was administered to a midshipman, the young officer would bend over a cannon and a cane would be used instead of the cat.

Further evidence against the nautical origin can be had by looking at early uses of the phrase *over a barrel*. The phrase only dates to 1939, first appearing in Raymond Chandler's novel *The Big Sleep*.

So, to what does the phrase allude if not a nautical origin? Most likely it is in an allusion to a drowning victim being stretched out over a barrel to clear his or her lungs. [10]

Mind Your Ps and Qs

Oftentimes, the nautical origin in question shares the stage with other explanations. The phrase *mind your Ps and Qs* has several popular folk etymologies, including a nautical candidate. The phrase dates to the late eighteenth century—at least 1779—which, unlike some of the other alleged nautical origins we have seen, makes an origin during the age of sail chronologically possible. But the evidence is lacking and the exact origin is unknown.

The nautical origin proposes that the *P* refers to a sailor's pea jacket and the *Q* refers to a sailor's pigtail, or queue. On board ship, fresh water was in short supply and washing was often neglected. As a result, sailors' hair would become greasy and dirty. The phrase was a reminder to sailors that when wearing their dress uniforms, they should be careful to ensure that their queues did not stain their pea jackets. As to evidence for this proposed origin, there is none. It is true that *pea* and *queue* were words in nautical parlance, but the early uses of the phrase *mind your Ps and Qs* are not in nautical contexts.

The only evidence that seems to support the nautical explanation is a single citation from 1602, appearing in Thomas Dekker's *Satiro-mastix*: "Now thou art in thy pee and cue." The phrase is rather cryptic. The *pee* is a reference to the coarse cloth used in pea jackets. The meaning of *cue* is uncertain. It could refer to a queue or pigtail (although *queue* meaning a pigtail is only known to date to 1748, nearly 150 years after Dekker wrote this).[11] It could also refer to cue meaning an appropriate course of action or to cue meaning disposition or humor. Dekker's use is not in a nautical context.

One non-nautical explanation is that the phrase is from *P and Q*, meaning *prime quality*. So to *mind your Ps and Qs* would mean to be exacting in detail and ensure high quality. This English dialectal usage dates to 1612, in *Knave of Harts* by Samuel Rowlands: "Bring in a quart of Maligo, right true: And looke, you/ Rogue, that it be Pee and Kew."

Another explanation is that the phrase originally refers to difficulty children had in learning to distinguish between the lowercase letters *p* and *q*, being mirror images of one another. To *learn one's Ps and Qs*, a phrase meaning to learn one's letters, is first recorded in 1820: "And I full five-and-twenty year Have always been school-master here; And almost all you know and see, Have learn'd their Ps and Qs from me."

This quotation is somewhat later than the phrase *mind your Ps and Qs*, which dates to at least 1779, but the explanation is not impossible as the origin. Often instead of children learning the alphabet this explanation is identified with printers distinguishing between a lowercase *p* and *q* in type. Letters in type are reversed and a *p* and *q* are easily confused, more so because they would be located in bins next to one another. But while this is a plausible explanation, there is no lexicographic evidence linking printers or printing to the phrase.[12]

Unlike the nautical explanation, the prime quality and learning the alphabet explanations have some lexicographic support. The phrase *P and Q* is found in these contexts in roughly the period that *mind your Ps and Qs* appears.

There are two other popular explanations that, like the nautical one, are unsupported by evidence. One links the phrase to the practice of maintaining a tally of drinks served in pubs and taverns. The following explanation appears in *Harper's New Monthly Magazine* in 1852:

Who ever knew, until comparatively late years, what was the origin of the cautionary saying, "Mind your P's and Q's?" A modern antiquarian, however, has put the world right in relation to that saying: In ale-houses, in the olden time, when chalk "scores" were marked upon the wall, or behind the door of the tap-room, it was customary to put the initials

"P" and "Q" at the head of every man's account, to show the
number of "pints" and "quarts" for which he was in arrears;
and we may presume many a friendly rustic to have tapped
his neighbor on the shoulder, when he was indulging too
freely in his potations, and to have exclaimed, as he pointed
to the chalk-score, "Mind your P's and Q's, man! Mind your
P's and Q's!"[13]

Sometimes this explanation is also given a nautical twist. It
is sailors in the pubs who are drinking and have to watch their
pints and quarts.

The final commonly suggested explanation is that it is a
variation on *mind your pleases and thank yous*, a plea for gentil-
ity and manners. There is no evidence to support this, nor does
the phrase *mind your pleases and thank yous* even exist outside of
explanations of the *Ps* and *Qs* origin.

Under the Weather

The phrase *under the weather*, meaning to be ill, is another
phrase that is commonly thought to be of nautical origin. On
the surface this makes sense. Mariners are very concerned with
the weather and to be beneath a storm is not a pleasant
prospect. A slightly different nautical explanation of the origin
of the phrase is a clipping of *under the weather bow*, the weather
bow being the side of a ship's bow that is taking the brunt of
rough seas. But neither explanation holds up under scrutiny.

Instead, this phrase is an Americanism that dates to 1827.
The contexts of early citations are not nautical at all. The
phrase probably comes from the idea that the weather can
affect one's mood and health.[14]

Knock Off

Many maritime aficionados claim that the term *knock off*, meaning to cease work, comes from oarsmen on a galley. The oarsmen would row to the beat of a drum, and when the drummer stopped beating the drum, or *knocked off*, the rowers could rest. Often Richard Henry Dana's 1840 book *Two Years Before the Mast* is used to justify this explanation. Dana uses *knock off* several times throughout the novel, such as the following from chapter XXIII: "After we had knocked off work and cleared up decks for the night . . ."

But again, the explanation does not hold water. *Knock off*, meaning to quit work, dates to the mid-seventeenth century and again, early uses are not nautical. The earliest is from George Daniel's 1649 *Trinarchodia (Henry V)* and refers not to the sea, but to the battle of Agincourt: "The Sun (who quafft French blood, to Harrie's health) knock's of / And can noe more."[15] Dana's use of *knock off* is simply use of a common term. Even though his book is about the sea, this term is not nautical.

Son of a Gun

Sometimes the nautical legends have been around for years and writings and citations can be found, some quite old, that seem to bear out the legendary origin. Such is the case with the phrase *son of a gun*. The nautical explanation is that in the age of sail, women, wives, mistresses, and prostitutes who were frequently on board ships in port or in home waters, would occasionally birth children aboard ship. Common sailors slept on the gun deck, and their wives and mistresses would sleep there too. So babies birthed on board were likely born on the gun deck. If male, such a child was referred to as a *son of a gun*.

In this case, the legend dates back to the mid-nineteenth century. As Admiral William Henry Smyth wrote in his 1867 book, the *Sailor's Word-book*, one of the primary sources for data on nineteenth-century nautical lingo: "Son of a gun, an epithet conveying contempt in a slight degree, and originally applied to boys born afloat, when women were permitted to accompany their husbands to sea; one admiral declared he literally was thus cradled, under the breast of a gun-carriage."

So the idea that the phrase has a nautical origin is quite old. The phrase *son of a gun*, however, is considerably older than this quote, dating to 1708. It first appears in the newspaper, *The British Apollo*: "You'r a Son of a Gun."[16]

Like *the devil to pay*, this phrase probably began life as a landsman's term, in this case a simple rhyming euphemism. It was later applied jocularly to children born afloat.

Railroad Origins

Enthusiasts of things nautical are not the only ones who promulgate false etymologies associated with their passion. While CANOE is a jocular acronym referring to alleged nautical origins, the phenomenon is not restricted to the sea. Any hobby or area of interest will generate stories of word and phrase origins. Railroads and railroad enthusiasts, for example, have their fair share of false origin stories. Two in particular appear again and again.

Balling the Jack

The first of these is the phrase *balling the jack*. It means to go fast. It appears for the first time in 1913 as the name of a lively ragtime tune and dance. It is likely from the fast pace of this song, but the origin is somewhat uncertain.[17] The phrase has been commonly used among railroad workers, but there is little evidence to indicate that the origin is from railroad jargon—it is more likely that the dance inspired the phrase and railroad workers picked it up and made it their own.

Balls to the Wall

The second of these alleged railroad phrases is the phrase *balls to the wall*, meaning an all-out effort. Like *balling the jack*, this phrase is often thought to have arisen from railroad work. The speed governor on train engines had round, metal weights at the end of arms. As the speed increased, the spinning balls would rise—being perpendicular to the walls at maximum speed. But there is no evidence to support this story. No use of the phrase is known to exist prior to the mid-1960s, and all the early cites are from military aviation, not railroads.

Like *freeze the balls off a brass monkey*, this phrase sounds as if it is a reference to a part of the male anatomy. In this case, however, the original usage has nothing to do with anatomy, coming rather from the world of aviation. The difference in the assessments of the two phrases is based on where the evidence takes us. In the case of *balls to the wall*, the early uses of the term do not appear to be anatomical references.

On an airplane, the handles controlling the throttle and the fuel mixture are often topped with ball-shaped grips, referred to by pilots as (what else?) *balls*. Pushing the balls forward, close to the front wall of the cockpit, results in the highest volume and richest mixture of fuel going to the engines and therefore the highest possible speed.

The earliest written known use of the phrase is from 1966-67 in Frank Harvey's *Air War—Vietnam*: "You know what happened on that first Doomsday Mission (as the boys call a big balls-to-the-wall raid) against Hanoi oil."[18]

The phrase may be a bit older. Several Korean War pilots have claimed that they used the phrase some fifteen years earlier, but definitive proof of these claims is lacking.

Ethnic Origins

Ah, of course! Kimono is come from the Greek word cheimas *is mean winter. So what do you wear in the wintertime to stay warm? A robe. You see, a robe, kimono, there you go.*
— Gus Portokalos, *My Big Fat Greek Wedding*[19]

Hobbies and interests are not the only sources of false origins. Ethnicity also arouses passions in people and these ethnic passions in turn generate linguistic urban legends. Like the character Gus in the movie *My Big Fat Greek Wedding*, many people want to ascribe word origins to their own ethnic heritage. A prime example is the belief that *the whole nine yards* refers to the amount of cloth needed to make a Scottish kilt. Few, however, go so far as Gus and claim such absurdities as a Japanese word being from Greek, but the pattern is a common one.

Lynch

An example of ethnic pride creating a false etymology is the word *lynch*, meaning a summary execution by a self-constituted court with no true legal authority. Many of Irish descent put forth the belief that the word is a reference to an incident that occurred in Galway, Ireland, in 1493. According to local lore, the mayor of Galway, James Lynch Fitz Stephen, hanged his own son for murder in that year. The proponents of the theory found an incident that matched the meaning of the word and ethnic pride took over. This just had to be the origin. The problem is that they did not actually look at the history of the word.

The ultimate origin of the verb *lynch* is reasonably well established. The term is American in origin, dating to shortly after the American Revolution. The term *lynch law* dates to 1811, first appearing in the writings of Andrew Ellicott: "Captain Lynch just mentioned was the author of the Lynch laws so well known and so frequently carried into effect some years ago in the southern States in violation of every principle of justice and jurisprudence." Ellicott is referring to a Captain William Lynch (1742–1820) of Pittsylvania, Virginia. Lynch led a self-created judicial tribunal during the American Revolution.

There are several other stories about the origin. One is that it is a reference to a Judge Charles Lynch, also from Virginia during the Revolutionary period. This Judge Lynch presided over the trials of Tory sympathizers, but there is no evidence to suggest that his trials were anything other than properly constituted proceedings. Another is that it is from Lynches Creek in South Carolina, which was a meeting place for vigilantes, ca. 1768.

The verb *to lynch* appears in 1836.[20] The Irish origin is simply not plausible, that the word would remain unpublished for over 300 years, only to pop up half a world away. There clearly has to be a more proximate Lynch who gave rise to the term, and Captain William Lynch is almost certainly the correct candidate.

Jazz

Jazz is often referred to as the only truly American art form. The origins of the term, however, have been a matter of debate for years. Like *OK* or *the whole nine yards*, there are multiple false etymologies suggested for *jazz*. Some of these are based on outdated scholarship rather than folklore. At one time they were legitimate theories, but have been proven wrong in recent years. Others are fueled by two infamous typographical errors in major reference works that falsely indicate the word *jazz* is older than it actually is. But some of the theories are just pure fancy.

Many of the competing origin stories claim an origin in African language, brought to America by slaves and applied to music by black musicians. Typically the word is said to come either from the Mandingo *jasi*, meaning to act out of character, or from the Temne *yas*, meaning to be energetic.

The hypothesis that jazz comes from an African word is a reasonable one given the large role that African Americans played in the development of the musical style, but in the end this hypothesis is not supported by the evidence. Still, this assumption is widespread and often stated in publications that should know better, such as *The Story of English*, by Robert Mc-Crum, Robert MacNeil, and William Cran:

> The name they gave to this new music was jazz. Originally the word was used by Blacks to mean speed up. The specific etymology of the word has never been pinpointed, but most scholars believe that it is of West African origin. By 1913, the word had moved into the mainstream of American culture, with both Blacks and Whites using jazz to mean a particular type of ragtime music with a syncopated rhythm.[21]

There is much wrong with this quote. *Jazz* did originally mean pep or to speed up, but it did not get its start in African-American English. Nor had the term entered the mainstream by 1913. In that year it remained an obscure, local term to most musicians, not to mention mainstream culture. Finally, until a few years ago most scholars might have acknowledged that a

West African origin was possible, but few would have stated it as a near certainty.

Often the African origin is connected with the American dialectal term *jasm*, meaning spirit, vigor, or energy. That word dates to 1860, appearing in J. G. Holland's *Miss Gilbert*:

> "She's just like her mother . . . Oh! She's just full of jasm!"
> "You've got the start of me . . . Now tell me what 'jasm' is."
> "If you'll take thunder and lightning, and a steamboat and a buzz-saw, and mix 'em up, and put 'em into a woman, that's jasm."[22]

The word *jasm* is of uncertain origin, but is likely related to *jism*, a word that dates to 1842 and can also mean energy or spirit, but can also mean semen. The sense meaning semen or sperm dates to at least 1854 and may be the original sense. The ultimate origin is unknown.[23] *Jasm*, in sense of vigor and pep as opposed to the sexual sense, may indeed be the ultimate origin of the *jazz*, but this has not been established.

One of the most infamous errors in the popular etymology of the word was committed by filmmaker Ken Burns in his PBS documentary mini-series about jazz. The Burns documentary and its accompanying book promulgated a patently wrong etymology of the word, although they did avoid the standard African origin story:

> As early as 1906, a San Francisco sportswriter was using the word to denote pep and enthusiasm on the baseball field, and there were those who thought it might have originally come from a West African word for speeding things up. But most authorities believe that the term, like the music, came from New Orleans—from the jasmine perfume allegedly favored by the city's prostitutes, or from "jezebel," a common nine-

teenth-century term for a prostitute, or as a synonym for sexual intercourse in Storyville, where some brothels were said to have been called "jay'n houses." "The original meaning of jazz was procreation," says the trumpet player Wynton Marsalis, "you can't get deeper or more profound than that unless you're contemplating the Creator."[24]

As we shall see, the word makes one of its earliest appearances in San Francisco baseball writing, but in 1913, not 1906. A few linguistic authorities point to a New Orleans origin, but none seriously consider an origin in *jasmine* or *Jezebel*. And Wynton Marsalis is a great musician, but he is not a credible authority on the subject of word origins. There is a sense of *jazz* meaning to engage in sexual intercourse, but this sense does not appear until 1918, after the musical sense had been firmly established.[25]

Finally, the Ken Burns documentary makes another error in indicating that the word was originally spelled *jass*. While the musical style was often spelled with a double S in the early years, the earliest spellings are with a double Z. All the photos in the documentary showing the *jass* spelling postdate the earliest known use of the word in 1913.

In addition to West African languages, the French word *jaser—meaning to speed up, to chatter, to make fun—*is sometimes cited as an origin in that the term can be associated with the musical style via the French spoken in New Orleans. The chief evidence for this French origin is a single 1831 use by Lord Palmerston referring to Talleyrand: "I am writing in the Conference, Matuszevic copying out a note for our signature, old Talley jazzing and telling stories to Lieven and Esterhazy and Wessenberg."[26] This is certainly a nonce variation on the French *jaser* and is unconnected with the later name for the musical style.

Finding the true etymology of jazz is complicated by several infamous errors, which keep recurring in popular accounts of the word's origin. Even the venerable *Oxford English Dictionary* makes an error here. The *OED* first cites the term as appearing in 1909 on a gramophone record titled *Uncle Josh in Society*.[27] This is an error; the recording is actually from 1919.[28] Also, two French dictionaries *Le Nouveau Petit Robert* (1993) and *Grand Larousse Dictionnaire de la Langue Francais* (1975) reference a 1908 use. These are typographical errors; they should read 1918.[29]

With all these incorrect hypotheses, folkloric tales, and errors, can we even know the true origin of *jazz*? The answer is yes. The true origin of the word was first put forward by San Francisco etymologist Peter Tamony in 1938. It has been discussed in several major reference works, including H. L. Mencken's *The American Language*. And recent research by etymologists Gerald Cohen, Barry Popik, and David Shulman have conclusively demonstrated Tamony's hypothesis to be correct.

Mencken succinctly summarizes Tamony's hypothesis in his 1948 Supplement 2 to *The American Language*:

> Tamony says that [jazz] was introduced to San Francisco in 1913 by William (Spike) Slattery, sports editor of the *Call*, and propagated by a band-leader named Art Hickman. It reached Chicago by 1915 but was not heard of in New York until a year later. . . . [In a note:] Slattery, according to Tamony, borrowed it from the vocabulary of crap-shooters and used it "as a synonym for ginger and pep," but it was soon used to designate Hickman's music, much to [Hickman's] disgust.[30]

Backing up Tamony's hypothesis, one of the first known uses of the word *jazz* appears in a March 3, 1913, baseball article in the *San Francisco Bulletin* by E. T. "Scoop" Gleeson:

McCarl has been heralded all along the line as a "busher," but now it develops that this dope is very much to the "jazz."

Three days later, Gleeson writes:

Everybody has come back to the old town full of the old "jazz" and [the San Francisco Seals] promise to knock the fans off their feet with their playing. What is the "jazz"? Why, it's a little of that "old life," the "gin-i-ker," the "pep," otherwise known as the enthusiasalum [*sic*]. A grain of "jazz" and you feel like going out and eating your way through Twin Peaks. [. . .] The team which speeded into town this morning comes pretty close to representing the pick of the army. Its members have trained on ragtime and "jazz" and manager Dell Howard says there's no stopping them.[31]

Gleeson used *jazz* in his baseball articles throughout the month of March 1913. Decades later, in 1938, Gleeson recalls the origin of *jazz*:

Similarly the very word "jazz" itself, came into general usage at the same time. We were all seated around the dinner table at Boyes [Springs, Sonoma County, the Seals spring training site,] and William ("Spike") Slattery, then sports editor of The Call, spoke about something being the "jazz," or the old "gin-iker fizz." "Spike" had picked up the expression in a crap game. Whenever one of the players rolled the dice he would shout, "Come on, the old jazz." For the next week we gave "jazz" a great play in all our stories. And when Hickman's orchestra swung into action for the evening's dances, it was natural to find it included as "the jazziest tune tooters in all the Valley of the Moon."[32]

Gleeson makes some errors of memory here. He used the term *jazz* in his articles for most of a month, not a week, and he is the only sportswriter to actually use it in print that month. It was not until the end of March that other writers began using the term. By April, it could be found throughout the San Francisco newspapers. His use of *jazziest* to describe Hickman's music is apparently in the sense of peppiest, and does not denote the style of music—that would come later.

Art Hickman is the key figure in developing the musical sense of *jazz* from the pep, vigor sense. In 1913 he was hired to put together a band for the Seals' entertainment during spring training. Another frequenter of the Seals' spring training camp was James Woods, manager of the St. Francis Hotel in San Francisco. After seeing Hickman at Boyes Springs, Woods gave him a regular job at the St. Francis, a gig that made Hickman one of the top orchestra leaders in the country. The word, popular among the Seals and their cadre of accompanying sportswriters, became associated with Hickman's ragtime music, evidently to Hickman's dismay.[33]

In 1914, Bert Kelly, a musician in Hickman's orchestra, moved east and started his own dance band in Chicago. In a 1957 letter to *Variety*, Kelly claims to be the first to use *jazz* to denote a style of music.[34] While this claim cannot be verified, it seems likely. The first use of the term in print to mean the style of music is from 1916.[35]

There is one monkey wrench to be thrown in this explanation. In the summer of 2003, researcher George Thompson found a citation of *jazz* that antedates Gleeson's use of the term. This earlier use, however, is still in a West Coast baseball context. The term appears in a April 2, 1912, *Los Angeles Times* article titled "Ben's Jazz Curve," about pitcher Ben Henderson:

"I got a new curve this year," softly murmured Henderson yesterday, "and I'm goin' to pitch one or two of them tomorrow. I call it the Jazz ball because it wobbles and you simply can't do anything with it."

As prize fighters who invent new punches are always the first to get their's [*sic*] Ben will probably be lucky if some guy don't hit that new Jazzer ball a mile today. It is to be hoped that some unintelligent compositor does not spell that the Jag ball. That's what it must be at that if it wobbles.[36]

Given this 1912 citation, it seems possible that Slattery did not pick up the term at a craps game as Gleeson suggests, but rather the word was floating around in West Coast baseball lingo at the time. Or perhaps Slattery did hear it at a craps game with baseball players.

So *jazz* began life as a San Francisco sportswriter's term for team spirit and aggressive play, possibly based on *jasm*, but this last cannot be conclusively established. The word was applied to the ragtime music of Art Hickman, whose band played at the San Francisco Seals' training camp. From there it traveled east with musicians until it eventually came to be associated with the new style of music coming out of New Orleans.

America

Another example of ethnic pride giving rise to false word origin stories is the name of the New World, *America*. Most people know that America is named after Amerigo Vespucci, but few know why.

Vespucci made two trips to the New World as a ship's navigator, the first in 1499, and the second in 1501. Then in 1503 and 1504 he published two letters he had written to Lorenzo de Medici. In the letters he put forward the idea that what Columbus had discovered was not in fact a new route to Asia, but rather a new continent. Vespucci published these letters under the title *Novus Mundus*, or *New World*, thereby coining that phrase. The letters were media hits and Vespucci became a celebrity, probably as much because of his description of the sex lives of American Indians as his innovative geographical theory.

In 1507, the cartographer Martin Waldseemüller published a map that designated the New World as *America*. This is the first known use of *America* as the name of the new lands across the Atlantic. Waldseemüller writes of this naming: "I do not see what is to hinder us from calling it Amerigé or America [. . .] after its discoverer Americus, a man of sagacious mind, since both Europe and Asia have got their names in feminine form."

The name *America* caught on very quickly and by 1515 it was widely used throughout Europe as the proper name for the New World. The speed with which the name caught on has caused some to question whether the Waldseemüller map was indeed the first use of the name.[37]

So, America is named after the man who first recognized that it was a new continent and not just a part of Asia. This is rather fitting actually, but this explanation is not accepted by all. Two major contenders, both championed in the name of ethnic pride, vie for the honors, but there is precious little evidence to support these contending theories.

The first of these is that the name *America* is from a Native American word. This theory was first advanced by Jules Marcou in a March 1875 article in *The Atlantic Monthly*. Marcou was struck by the name of the Amerrique Mountains and the Amerrique people of Nicaragua. Marcou became convinced that this had to be the origin of the name. His chief evidence being that the *–ique* or *–ic* ending is a common one for place names in the Lenea language of Central America.[38]

Marcou argued that Columbus had met the Amerrique Indians on his fourth voyage to the New World and that he had probably carried the name back with him. Columbus did visit the coastal region of Nicaragua that is now home to the Amerrique Indians and he certainly had some contact with the people living there at the time. But if he acquired the name *America* from this source there is no record of it. Columbus never used the word or anything like it—a fact that Marcou acknowledges.[39]

So how do we account for this? It is possible that the similarity is sheer coincidence? The answer is yes. Out of all the native languages and names, at least one is bound to be similar to *America* in form and pronunciation. If it were not a mountain range and a people of Nicaragua, it would be something else in another Native American language. Further, the pronunciation and spelling of a native name could very well be influenced by the European name *America*. So by the late nineteenth century, *Amerrique* looked and sounded very similar to *America*, even if 400 years before it had been rather different. Finally, the name *Amerrique* may not be native at all, but rather an import from Europe. The natives may have been called this because they lived in *America*. This last may very well be true because the native name *Amerrique* is not recorded until nearly 370 years after Waldseemüller drew his map.

The name *Amerrique* is not even attested to until 1874, only a year before Marcou came up with his theory, when an English scientist named Thomas Belt mapped the region. Belt did not coin the name, but used a local one, whose origin is a mystery. For his part, Belt wrote Marcou in 1878 and stated it was his belief that the similarity was a coincidence.[40]

The second legend is one that is common in Britain and appeals to Anglo-Saxon and Welsh ethnic pride. It holds that *America* is named after a fifteenth-century Bristol merchant and official named Richard Ameryk (also spelled *ap Meryke* and *Amerike*) who had some tenuous connection with Cabot's 1497 and 1498 voyages during which the continent of North America was discovered. Exactly what role Ameryk played in Cabot's expeditions is not known for certain, but it had something to do with finance. Ameryk is known to have authorized the payment of Cabot's pension to his family.

The Ameryk hypothesis was first put forward in 1908 by Alfred E. Hudd, a Bristol historian. The chief evidence for this hypothesis, which Hudd himself labeled as mere speculation, are Bristol city records said to have been published in 1497. Allegedly, the records use the name *America* in reference to Cabot's voyage before Vespucci made his first voyage to the New World and a decade before Waldseemüller published his map: "This year, on St. John the Baptist's day [24 June 1497], the land of America was found by the merchants of Bristowe, in a ship of Bristowe called the 'Mathew,' the which said ship departed from the port Bristowe the 2nd of May and came home again the 6th August following."

The problem is that this was not written in 1497. The original 1497 records have long been lost. This quote is from a 1565 summary of the Bristol city records for 1497. It was written well after the name *America* was in common use, and thus it is not at all surprising that the New World is called *America* in this account. In addition, not only have the original records been destroyed, but the 1565 manuscript is gone too, destroyed in an 1860 fire. All we have are modern accounts of a lost manuscript that describes another, earlier, lost manuscript.[41]

There is considerable evidence that English fishermen from Bristol made regular voyages across the Atlantic to fish the

Grand Banks and established fishing camps on the North American coastline well before Columbus made his famous voyages or Cabot got credit for discovering North America. But there is absolutely no evidence to indicate the word *America*, or anything similar to it, was used by Bristol fishermen or merchants to refer to the New World until Waldseemüller created his famous map. The connection to Ameryk is simply assumed because the names resemble one another, and because he was a resident of Bristol and had a connection to Cabot's voyage.

The Ameryk legend also displays another characteristic about many false word origin legends: The word is one named after a person, an eponymous origin story.

chapter /'cHaptər/ Five

Hookers, Harlots,
and Condoms

N o, this chapter is not about what you may think it is. Instead it is about false eponyms, or false stories that ascribe a word's origin to the name of a person. Like all three of
the words in this chapter's title, there are many linguistic urban
legends that give the name of a person, either real or fictional,
as the putative origin of a word.

One thing that complicates the debunking of such legends
is that, unlike pre-twentieth-century acronyms, many words do
indeed come from the name of a person. The legend of America, Vespucci, and Richard Ameryk discussed in the last chapter clearly demonstrates this problem (chapter 4, p. 126). In this
case, the legend is eponymous, but so is the true origin.

While eponymous legends are sometimes deceptive due to
the number of true eponyms, they are also often easy to de-

bunk. If the word can be shown to exist before the alleged namesake was born or achieved fame, then the legend is clearly not true.

Hooker

One such legend that can be easily debunked is the one surrounding the word *hooker,* meaning prostitute. It is commonly said to come from the name of the U.S. Civil War general "Fighting Joe" Hooker. Hooker commanded the Army of the Potomac for five months in 1863. His men were a rowdy bunch, and his headquarters was well known as a den of iniquity. Charles Francis Adams, Jr., grandson of John Quincy Adams and great-grandson of John Adams, said Hooker's headquarters was "a place where no self-respecting man liked to go, and no decent woman could go. It was a combination of barroom and brothel."[1]

While "Fighting Joe" may not have been a man of upstanding moral character, he did not lend his name to the oldest profession. The word *hooker* was used to mean prostitute at least a full fifteen years prior to the start of the Civil War. N. E. Eliason in *Tarheel Talk* records that the term was used in North Carolina as early as 1845: "If he comes by way of Norfolk he will find any number of pretty Hookers in the Brick row not far from French's hotel."[2]

John Russell Bartlett in the 1859 edition of his *Dictionary of Americanisms* also lists the term. Bartlett defines the word as "A resident of the Hook; i.e. a strumpet, a sailor's trull. So called from the number of houses of ill-fame frequented by sailors at the Hook (i.e., Corlear's Hook) in the city of New York."[3] So, if *hooker* is not named after the Civil War general, where does the word come from? Most modern sources discount Bartlett's connection between *hooker* and Corlear's Hook due to lack of evidence and because of the earlier citation from North Carolina, but there are other possibilities.

Hooker is also British slang for a thief dating to the sixteenth century. A prostitute's penchant for supplementing her income with a little thievery on the sly could have led to the application of the term *hooker*. It is also a slang term for an old boat (from the Dutch *hoecker-schip*, or fishing boat).[4] This could be the origin, similar to *tramp*, as in *tramp steamer*. But the most probable explanation is that a prostitute is one that hooks or snares clients.

But we should not let old Fighting Joe completely off the hook, as it were. Like Old Kinderhook and *OK* or, as we shall see a bit later on in this chapter, Thomas Crapper and *crap*, General Hooker and his nocturnal habits undoubtedly played a role in popularizing the term. *Hooker* is what some linguists call an aptronym, a word that is aptly associated with the name of a person but not named for that individual.

Harlot

Debunking the legend of *hooker* is relatively easy. Since General Hooker did not become famous until the Civil War, the 1845 citation, some fifteen years before the war, conclusively debunks the legend. But if the namesake lived or became famous before the first known appearance of a term, the debunking can be trickier. In these cases we cannot rely on simple chronology. Such is the case with *harlot*.

The legend is that *harlot* is an eponym for Arlette, the unmarried mother of William the Conqueror. It is an old tale, first suggested ca. 1570 by William Lambarde, an Elizabethan historian. Arlette, also known as Herleva, was the daughter of Fulbert, a tanner in Falaise, Normandy. Robert, the Duke of Normandy, saw her bathing in a river one day and decided she was the woman for him, at least for the moment. He took her as his mistress and their union produced William, who as an adult would conquer England. It is an interesting and true tale, but it is not the origin of the word *harlot*.

Instead, *harlot* comes from the Old French *herlot*, and use of the term in English dates to sometime after 1225, not all that long after the Norman Conquest. The chronology would seem to lend some credence to the Arlette story, but in this case the key to the debunking is the original sense of the word. *Harlot* did not originally mean a wanton woman. Rather, both the Old French root and the early appearances of the word in English use the word to mean a vagabond or beggar, a rascal or knave. The earliest uses of *harlot* are all in reference to men. By the mid-fourteenth century the connotations associated with the word had changed, and *harlot* was being used in a positive sense and applied to jesters, buffoons, jugglers, or any man of good cheer. It was in this sense that Chaucer described the Sumonour in the Prologue to his *Canterbury Tales*, ca.1386: "He was a gentil harlot and a kynde, / A bettre felawe sholde men noght fynde."

Interestingly, the original derogatory sense had not faded by Chaucer's day, as this passage from the Reeve's Tale shows: "Ye false harlot, quod the Millere hast?" Originally, *harlot* only referred to men and it was not until the fifteenth century that the word was applied to women. The word gradually became associated with actors, other entertainers, and eventually to prostitutes. The narrowing of the meaning to the modern sense of a wanton woman or prostitute is in large part due to English translations of the Bible. Sixteenth-century translations, such as the Geneva Bible of 1560, began using *harlot* where Wyclif's earlier translation had used words like strumpet and whore.[5] This Biblical use eventually drove the other senses of the word out of the language.

Condom

Both Fighting Joe Hooker and Arlette of Normandy were real people, even if the tales about their inspiring the coining of words are false. Sometimes, however, the person is fabricated along with the eponymous legend.

An example of this is the legend that says the *condom* was named for its inventor, a British physician who lived during the reign of Charles II (1660–85). There is no direct evidence that any such Dr. Condom existed, and the origin of the word is unknown, but that has not stopped the spread of the legend. The hunt is made difficult by the variations in the spelling of the word (quondam, condon, etc.) and the fact that respectable dictionaries and reference works did not include such words until very recently. The *Oxford English Dictionary*, for example, did not include *condom* until 1972, even though the *OED*'s files held an 1888 letter to James Murray, that dictionary's famed editor, containing the earliest known citation of the term's use.

This first known use of the term was in a 1705 letter referring to John Campbell, the second Duke of Argyll, who traveled from London to Edinburgh bringing with him a "certaine instrument called a Quondam, q$^{ch.}$ occasioned ye debauching of a great number of Ladies of qualitie, and oy^r young gentlewomen."

Argyll was a strong advocate of the union between England and Scotland that would be known as the United Kingdom. As such he had many political enemies. Among them was John Hamilton, the second Baron of Bellhaven, who penned the following poem in 1706 referring to Argyll and his device, the first appearance of the word in a published source:

When Reasoning's answer'd
By seconded Votes,
And speeches are banter'd
By outfield turn-coats,
Then Sirenge and Condum
Come both in request,
While virtuous Quondam
Is treated in Jest.[6]

The word *condom* is associated with the name of its inventor as early as 1708. This association first appears in an anonymous poem titled *Almonds for Parrots*:

a Gut the Learn'd call, Blind;
'Till Condon, for the great invention fam'd,
Found out its Use, and after him 'twas nam'd.[7]

The following year, the claim that the prophylactic was named for its inventor is repeated in the newspaper *The Tatler*, which records the following account of his appearance in Will's Coffee House, a famed gathering place for writers, satirists, and wits, on May 13, 1709. Although this account does not mention the inventor by name:

[T]here are considerable Men appear in all Ages, who, for some eminent Quality or Invention, deserve the Esteem and

Thanks of the Publick. Such a Benefactor is a Gentleman of the [Coffee-] House, who is observ'd by the Surgeons with much Envy; for he has invented an Engine for the Prevention of Harms by Love-Adventures, and has, by great Care and Application, made it an Immodesty to name his Name. This Act of Self-denial has gain'd this worthy Member of the Commonwealth a great Reputation. Some Law-givers have departed from their Abodes for ever, and commanded the Observation of their Laws till their Return; others have us'd other Artifices to fly the Applause of their Merit; but this Person shuns Glory with greater Address, and has by giving his Engine his own Name, made it obscene to speak of him more. However, he is rank'd among, and receiv'd by the modern Wits, as a Promoter of Gallantry and Pleasure.[8]

In 1724 the inventor is first identified as a physician. Daniel Turner, in his *Syphilis. A Practical Dissertation on the Venereal Disease* writes:

Dr. Sharp, as well as the Wolverhampton Surgeon, with two or three others behind the Curtain, stand Candidates with Dr. C—n, for the Glory of the invention.[9]

Unfortunately for those of us trying to trace the development of the word, Turner bowdlerizes the name. It is probably *Condon*, but this is by no means certain. In 1728, the doctor is referred to as a colonel. Over the next few centuries various accounts refer to him as either a physician or a colonel.

All this would make it seem that such a person did in fact exist. But there is a major problem with the story, namely that no one has identified an actual person who is a logical or likely candidate. Numerous scholars have searched high and low for candidates named Condom, Condon, or something similar, to no avail.

Condum, Cundum, and Gondom simply are not English names. No one with these names appears in any histories or records of the period. There are names like Condon and Compton, but while people with these names can be found, none appear to be likely candidates. No record of a physician, surgeon, military officer, peer of the realm, member of philosophical societies, or known inventor from the period with these names has been found.

Two possibilities for an eponym still exist. The man could have been a person of no status or he could have been a foreigner. Both are unlikely. A person of no social rank would not have been frequenting Wills Coffee House or hobnobbing with the nobility as the tales suggest. The early accounts treat him as a person of worth, not as a nobody. The other is that the inventor was not British and the name was imported to Britain ca. 1700. This is also unlikely. The word makes its first appearance in English and accounts of the period show that the name of the device was first used in Britain and only later crossed the channel to the Continent. More likely, the story about an inventor named Condom or Condon is simply a fiction and the references to him are merely satire.

So, if not an eponym where does the word come from? There are other, non-eponymous, suggestions for the origin of *condom*. Three are commonly cited. None of them have any significant supporting evidence, and all must be classified as speculation:

- It is named after the village of Condom in southern France. This hypothesis was first proposed in 1904. Other than the similarity in form and the general English association with all things erotic to France, there is nothing to suggest that this is in fact the origin.
- It is from the Latin *condus*, meaning that which preserves, a reference to the device's original use for preventing syphilis.

- It is from the Persian *kondü* or *kendü*, an earthen vessel for storing grain. This is a reference to the sheath's function as a receptacle for semen. It supposedly made its way into English via Greek and Latin.

While the good Dr. Condom is almost certainly fictional, the usual pattern in linguistic legendry is to find a real personage on which to hang the eponym. Sometimes, as in the case of *hooker*, an aptly named person is the source of the legend. A coincidence where the name is similar to the word in question gives rise to the tale.

Crap

Such is the case with Thomas Crapper and the word *crap*. Crapper, as the legend would have it, invented the flush toilet and in so doing gave his name to posterity. The legend is, at least in part, true.

Unlike the mysterious Dr. Condom, there really was a Thomas Crapper. He was an English sanitary engineer and inventor who lived from 1837–1910. He did not, however, "invent" the flush toilet, nor does the word *crap* come from his name. Crapper is also often falsely credited with inventing the "Silent Valveless Water Waste Preventer," a type of toilet that could effectively flush when the tank was half full. Crapper owned a plumbing supply company and sold this device. He may have even bought the patent rights from the real inventor, Albert Giblin, but he did not invent it.[10]

The word *crap*, meaning excrement, is from the Old French, via Middle English, *crappe*, meaning husks of grain or chaff. The word ultimately comes from the Medieval Latin *crappa*. English use dates to the mid-fifteenth century.[11] Over the centuries the meaning of the word changed, from chaff, to refuse and leavings, and eventually to excrement. The earliest known use of *crap* to mean excrement is from 1846, in the form *crapping ken*, an outhouse or water closet: "Where's the plant, cully?" . . . "Fenced, in a dunniken." . . . "What? Fenced in a crapping ken?"[12]

Since Crapper was only nine years old in 1846, his name is obviously not the origin of the word. This is a case where an appropriately named man made a contribution to the relevant field, an aptronym, not an eponym.

But as with Old Kinderhook and *OK* or General Hooker and *hooker*, Thomas Crapper probably helped popularize the word *crap*. His plumbing company manufactured thousands of toilets and other fixtures, many bearing his name. This undoubtedly strengthened the connection between excrement and the word *crap*.

In the case of *crap*, the legend was further popularized and strengthened by an infamous book. In 1969, writer Wallace Reyburn published a book that mistakenly credits Crapper with both the origin of the word *crap* and the invention of the toilet. This book, *Flushed with Pride: The Story of Thomas Crapper* is a light-hearted romp that, while factual in some respects, tends to sacrifice the truth for wit and humor. Many recent accounts of the legend source this book, giving the tale a veneer of credibility.

There is another false eponymous origin related to the word *crap*, only to a different sense of the word. The game of *craps* is etymologically unrelated to the word meaning excrement, but shares a similar eponymous legend about its origin. In this case the word is attributed to Bernard de Marigny, a New Orleans gambler, ca. 1800, known as *Johnny Crapaud*, literally Johnny Toad. Like the story of Thomas Crapper, this one can be debunked by simply examining the chronology. Marigny's appearance is too early to be the source of the name of the game of *craps*.

Instead, *craps* is a corruption of *crab*. In the eighteenth century, *crabs* was an English slang term for a low roll of dice, first spoken by Lord Carlisle in 1768: "If you . . . will play, the best thing I can wish you is, that you may win and never throw crabs."

Why the English called such a toss *crabs* is not known. By 1843, the word had corrupted into *craps* and had come to denote the name of the dice game.[13]

In Like Flynn

Another phrase that is usually associated with a real person is *in like Flynn*, meaning that one is in favor, that success is assured. In this case, the origin of the phrase is unknown; and while the legend could be true, the evidence indicates that it is probably not.

This phrase is commonly thought to be a reference to the ease with which movie star Errol Flynn bedded women. More specifically, many believe it to date from Flynn's 1942–43 statutory rape trial, in which he was acquitted. It has been associated with him since at least 1946, when an article in *American Speech* gives the phrase as a term in World War II Air Force slang:

> IN LIKE FLYNN. Everything is O.K. In other words the pilot is having no more trouble than Errol Flynn has in his cinematic feats.[14]

It is clear from other evidence, however, that the phrase does not stem from the 1942–43 rape trial. Etymologist Barry Popik has found several uses of the phrase prior to Flynn's trial. One as early as July 1940, in reference to a party of people being told they would have access to the New York World's Fair: "Your name is Flynn. . . you're in." [15]

In February 1942, a year before Flynn is acquitted of the rape charges, the phrase appears on the other side of the country in San Francisco:

> Answer these questions correctly and your name is Flynn, meaning you're in, provided you have two left feet and the written consent of your parents. [16]

Furthermore, the sexual connotations of the phrase do not clearly appear until the 1970s. Some of the avoidance of sexual connotation could be a result of editorial discretion, where the sexual meaning of the slang was avoided in published works, but still the early citations are used in distinctly non-sexual contexts, such as gaining entry to the World's Fair. It is possible that the phrase refers to Errol Flynn as he was famous long before the rape trial, but the evidence is stacking up against it.

Another eponymous theory links the phrase with Edward J. "Boss" Flynn (1892–1953), a Democratic machine politician from the Bronx. The phrase in this tale is a reference to the fact that Flynn's candidates always won. The date of the phrase's appearance fits with this explanation, but other than plausible chronology there is no solid evidence of a connection.

In the end, the phrase, despite being a reference to a name, may not be eponymous at all. *In like Flynn* may simply be rhyming slang, originally not referring to any specific individual. Barry Popik has turned up the following from a February 1943 newspaper column in which the journalist is speculating on the origin of the phrase:

Seems as though my guess about the derivation of the phrase, "I'm Flynn" wasn't altogether correct. I said it meant one was all set, ready, fixed, etc.—and that's right. But two correspondents, O. B. and John O'Reilly agree that it began with some such phrase as "Well, I'm in like Flynn." Finally, you were "in, Flynn." Now it's just "I'm Flynn." The reverse of the phrase is not common, but it started with "I'm out like Stout," which was shortened to "out, Stout" and is now "I'm Stout" (meaning things aren't so good).[17]

Rather than being named for Errol Flynn, it appears likely that the phrase got its start as rhyming slang, became associated with the actor in the early 1940s, probably facetiously during his trial, and afterward could not shake the association with the actor because of his fame.

Real McCoy

This is a rather common occurrence where words or phrases are obviously related to a name. People who do not know the true namesake often create their own stories, associating the word or phrase with a person who is more famous than the true namesake. Another example of this is the case of the *real Mc-Coy*, a phrase meaning the genuine article, the true thing. Few know who the *real McCoy* really is. One story vies for top honors in the popular imagination.

Many claim that the term derives from Norman Selby (ca. 1873–1940), a notorious American boxing champion who fought under the name Charles "Kid" McCoy. Selby started boxing professionally in 1890, winning the middleweight title in 1897. Fighting as a heavyweight in 1900, he lost a fight against James J. "Gentleman Jim" Corbett and was widely thought to have thrown the fight. Selby continued to box until 1916. In 1924, Selby's lover, Theresa Mors, was found shot to death in their home. He was convicted of manslaughter and served about ten years at San Quentin Penitentiary in California. He committed suicide in 1940.

In the ring, Selby/McCoy was known for his theatrics, often feigning illness in the weeks before a fight only to appear in the ring strong and fit. He is also widely credited with inventing the corkscrew punch, a punch thrown while rotating the fist, causing cuts on the opponent's face.

Misinformation about Selby is rife. Sources differ on such basic facts as the year of his birth, how many times he was married (he is known to have married at least six different women and married one woman three different times), whether or not he won the welterweight title (he did win the middleweight title), and how many years he served in prison. He was a larger-than-life figure, and it is hard to define where truth leaves off and exaggeration begins.[18]

There are two different stories about how "Kid McCoy" was dubbed *the real McCoy*. In one, Selby gets into a fight with a drunk who refuses to believe he is the famous boxer. After being knocked down with one punch, the drunk declares that he was indeed "the real McCoy." In the other story, McCoy is given the moniker by sportswriters, who claim they never know who will show up at a fight, the "real" champion, or the man who feigns illness and throws fights.

Alternatively, it is often suggested that the term derives from Elijah McCoy (1843–1929), who invented a type of hydrostatic lubricator in 1872. And while other McCoys are sometimes put forth as the inspiration for the phrase, these two are cited most often.

But if not from either of these men, who is the real *real Mc-Coy*? The phrase dates to 1856 and comes from a brand of whisky distilled by G. Mackay and Co.:

A drappie o' the real McKay

The distiller officially adopted the phrase as an advertising slogan in 1870. Figurative use of the phrase begins with Robert Louis Stevenson in an 1883 letter:

For society, there isnae sae muckle; but there's myself—the auld Johnstone, ye ken—he's the real Mackay, whatever.

The whisky origin is strengthened by later use of the word *McCoy* to mean high-quality spirits, as in the 1908 quote from Davenport's *Butte & Montana:*

I took a good-sized snort out of that big bottle in the middle and I declare I thought I was going to throw up my guts during the first hymn. Have you none of the clear McCoy handy around the house?

There is also this entry in O'Brien & Stephens's 1911 *Australian Slang:*

Mackay, the real: pronounced Muckeye: slang term to denote absolute genuineness or purity. A dram of really good spirits would be spoken of as "a drop of the real Mackay."

Finally, while quite a bit later, there is this prohibition-era quote from Witwer's 1923 *Fighting Blood:*

'At's the real McCoy you got there, brother . . . comes right down from Canada![19]

In contrast, the earliest known association of the term with the boxer is from the *Los Angeles Times* in September 1904:

If "Kid" McCoy's real name is Selby, then he is not "the real McCoy," after all.[20]

The phrasing of this quote indicates that the writer was applying a known phrase to McCoy and his reason for doing so was the boxer's use of a pseudonym, not for either of the legendary stories.

There is a claim that the May 25, 1899, edition of the *San Francisco Examiner* uses the term *the real McCoy* in reference to the boxer, but inspection of microfilmed copies of the paper fails to turn up the phrase.[21] Other uses of the phrase in reference to the boxer occur throughout the rest of the boxer's career, such as this one from a Nevada newspaper article from 1914:

"Kid" McCoy, the one and original real McCoy, is on his way to Reno.[22]

The use of "original" in this article shows that the term was in general use and could mean other things, not just the boxer. What we have here is an early association of an existing phrase with the boxer.

The 1883 Stevenson quote demonstrates that the term was in figurative use, albeit with the *Mackay* spelling, when the boxer Selby was still a child. The McCoy spelling does not appear until 1901, again in a British source: "Giving it a good ring to show it was the real McCoy."[23]

This 1901 quotation that uses the *McCoy* spelling is contemporaneous with the boxer's prime fighting days, but it is not a reference to the boxer or even to the sport. This coupled with the earlier Stevenson quote and the whisky sense makes the eponym for the boxer an unlikely origin.

Though the inventor Elijah McCoy was alive and famous by 1883, the earlier Scottish use for the whisky, which undoubtedly was the inspiration for Stevenson's use of the term, antedates his fame as well. While neither of these two are the origin of the term, Selby and Elijah McCoy probably influenced and standardized the change in spelling from Mackay to McCoy.

Dixie

Stories of eponymous origins are not always false. Often the word in question is indeed an eponym, only popularly attributed to the wrong person. At the end of the last chapter, we saw how America was an eponym for one man, but it also had a legend associating it with another. This is not the only case of this in American toponymy. The term *Dixie*, used to refer to the American South, is named after one man and often credited to another.

The earliest recorded use of the term *Dixie* is in the song *Johnny Roach*, written by Daniel D. Emmett, a blackface minstrel singer originally from Ohio. The song was first performed in February 1859:

Gib me de place called Dixie Land,
Wid hoe and shubble in my hand.

Emmett also wrote the more famous song *Dixie's Land* that immortalized the term, which he first performed in April of the same year:

I wish I was in de land ob cotton,
Old times dar am not forgotten,
Look away! Look away! Look away! Dixie Land.
In Dixie Land whar' I was born in,
Early on one frosty mornin',
Look away! Look away! Look away! Dixie Land.

While there is no recorded use of the term prior to Emmett's songs, there are attestations by people who recall the term being used before 1859. And Emmett himself never claimed to have originated the word, saying that it was one he had heard in use:

> "Dixie's Land" is an old phrase applied to the Southern States . . . lying south of Mason and Dixon's line. In my traveling days amongst the showmen, when we would start for a winter's season south, while speaking of the change, they would invariably ejaculate [*sic*] the stereotyped saying—"I Wish I was in Dixie's Land," meaning the southern country.[24]

So if Emmett did not coin the term, where did it come from? Most likely, the term is simply a reference to the Mason-Dixon Line, the border between Pennsylvania and Maryland that separated the slave states from the free states. The Penn and Calvert families that were the proprietors of the two colonies had long disputed where the border lay. As a compromise, in 1763 they appointed astronomers Charles Mason and Jeremiah Dixon to survey the border. By 1773 the line had been run all the way to the end of Maryland's northern border. The survey continued until 1779, completing the portion of the southern border of Pennsylvania that bordered Virginia (now West Virginia).

By the 1830s the term *Mason and Dixon* had come to figuratively denote the boundary between the slave and free states. Somewhere in the transition from meaning the boundary to denoting the southern states, *Mason* was lost and all that remained was *Dixie*.

But *Dixie* has other, false, eponymous origins. It is sometimes claimed that the term is a reference to Johan Dixie (sometimes spelled Dixy), a Manhattan slave owner of the late-eighteenth and early-nineteenth centuries. Dixie, according to the myth, was kind to his slaves, but they were eventually sold into the South, either when Dixie died or when New York abolished slavery—the tale varies in the telling. Dixie's former slaves spread stories about how good life was in "Dixie's Land" up north. While it is deliciously ironic to think that *Dixie* first referred to New York City, there is no evidence to indicate that this is the origin or even true.

The second of these false eponymous origins dates to 1951 when Mitford Mathews uncovered evidence of a minstrel performer named Dixey who played in Philadelphia (and presumably elsewhere) in 1856. Mathews speculates that Emmett probably knew the man and that this could be the origin, but says more evidence is needed.[25] While speculation is tempting, the hypothesis does not square with Emmett's own account of how he encountered the term.

In addition to the false eponymous origins, there are other false origin stories for *Dixie* that have nothing to do with a person's name. The first of these links the term to the French *dix* meaning ten. The Citizen's Bank of Louisiana issued bilingual, ten-dollar banknotes that bore that French word. These notes circulated widely in the South before the Civil War and were a common form of currency. The problem with this hypothesis is that no reference to *dixies* as the plural for banknote has been found, nor was the term associated with banknotes in the region until modern times.

And yet another story claims New York City as the origin for *Dixie*, this time as a children's game. In 1872, the magazine *New York Weekly* claimed that *Dixie's Land* was a term used in games of tag since the late eighteenth century.[26] William Wells Newell in his 1883 *Games and Songs of American Children* repeats this claim:

> A boundary line marks out "Tom Tidler's Ground," [. . .] This Eldorado has many different local names—Van Diemen's land in Connecticut; Dixie's Land in New York, an expression which antedates the war.

As in *Ring Around the Rosie* (see chapter 1, p. 24), however, Newell does not provide any evidence to substantiate the earlier date; and in his detailed description, Newell provides evidence that militates against pre–Civil War play of this game:

> A line having been drawn, to bound "Dixie's Land," the players cross the frontier with the challenge:
>
>> On Dixie's land I'll take my stand,
>> And live and die in Dixie.[27]

The use of lyrics from a version of Emmett's song in the game would indicate that the children's use of the term in New York does not in fact antedate the Civil War or Emmett's song.

Upset

Not all eponyms are inspired by the names of humans. Occasionally, animals inspire the coining of words. Two particular etymological urban legends are about the names of famous horses. The first of these is not quite properly classified as an urban legend. Until quite recently, it was a legitimate hypothesis for the origin of the term. Recent scholarship, however, has disproved it.

The term in question is the sports term, *upset*, meaning an unexpected defeat of one favored to win. The story is that this use of the word stems from a classic horse race that pitted Man o' War, one of the greatest racehorses of all time, against an unlikely opponent named Upset.

During his career, Man o' War lost only one race, the August 13, 1919, Stanford Memorial at Saratoga. Man o' War was heavily favored to win, but lost to Upset. This, the legend goes, is where the sports term *upset* comes from. Man o' War would face Upset in five other races, winning every one, but this one loss early in his career would be the one to make lexicographic history.

Many lexicographers and etymologists thought the story too good to be true, but no one could disprove it. Sporting usages of *upset* prior to 1919 just could not be found. Then in late 2002, researcher George Thompson, using the newly available tools of full-text searching of the *New York Times* computer databases, turned up a string of sporting usages of *upset* dating back to the mid-nineteenth century. Thompson traced the sporting use of the verb *to upset* to September 13, 1865:

> The racing was of the highest order; the contests being close and exciting, and the judgment of the knowing ones fairly upset by the unexpected results.

The use of *upset* as a noun appears in the *New York Times* on July 17, 1877:

The programme for to-day at Monmouth Park indicates a
victory for the favorite in each of the four events, but racing
is so uncertain that there may be a startling upset.[28]

Thompson found numerous uses of the term in late-
nineteenth-century sportswriting, proving beyond a doubt that
the word *upset* was a well-established sporting term by the time
Man o' War lost the infamous race. Upset did not sire a term,
like Thomas Crapper or Joe Hooker; he was just aptly named.

Pumpernickel

While the story of Upset is really a case of recent scholarship
disproving a previously viable hypothesis, the second of these
equine eponyms is a classic linguistic urban legend. It concerns
the word *pumpernickel,* the dark rye bread. The legend associ-
ates the name of the bread with Napoleon's horse, Nicol. According to the tale, while campaigning in Germany, Napoleon
was served the dark bread at a meal. Napoleon thought the
bread unfit for human consumption and declared: "C'est du
pain pour Nicol." (This is bread for Nicol.) *Pain pour Nicol,* as
the legend would have it, was subsequently corrupted into
pumpernickel.

Like *upset,* however, the word predates the horse and Napoleon. English use of the word *pumpernickel* dates to 1756, appearing in Thomas Nugent's travelogue of Europe, *The Grand
Tour:*

Their bread is of the very coarsest kind, ill baked, and as
black as a coal, for they never sift their flour. The people of
the country call it Pompernickel, which is only a corruption
of a French name given it by a gentleman of that nation,

who passed through this country. It is reported, that when this coarse bread was brought to table, hye looked at it and said, *Qu'il etoit bon pour Nickel,* That it was good for Nickel, which was the name of his horse. Those, however, who are used to it, are strong and robust.

This story predates Napoleon, who was born in 1769. And while the story about a horse named Nicol or Nickel is old, it is not the origin of *pumpernickel,* which is German, dating to 1663 in that language.[29]

Ellis Island Name Changing

Immigration Official: "What is your name? Come on son, what is your name?"
Translator: ["What is your name?" in Italian] then, looking at the tag on Vito's coat, "Vito Andolini from Corleone."
Immigration Official: "Corleone—Vito Corleone. Okay over there. Next—your name?"
                                        —The Godfather Part II [30]

Many people claim that the names of their ancestors were clipped or altered upon arrival at Ellis Island to make them more "American" and easier to spell and pronounce. The preceding quote from *The Godfather Part II* is a classic instance of this story. The question is, did this actually happen?

The answer is no, or at least it never happened in the ways commonly depicted in the tales. Immigration officials at Ellis Island and other ports of entry did not deliberately alter the names of immigrants. In fact, immigration regulations specifically prohibited officials from altering the names of those arriving in America—the chief concern of officials was the prohibition of the entry of undesirable aliens and this would be compromised if names were changed.

Typically the story told is much like the one depicted in *The Godfather*: the immigrant cannot speak English and the immigration officer cannot speak the immigrant's language. So the officer simply makes up a name and assigns it to the immigrant. This is false in several respects.

First, immigration officers usually did speak the language of the immigrant. The officers were usually immigrants themselves, hired specifically for their language skills, and were usually assigned to process immigrants from their own countries.

Second, immigration officers did not take down the names of immigrants. They received copies of the ships' manifests and simply checked the immigrants' names against those lists. Officials at Ellis Island and other ports of entry simply did not have the opportunity to change the names of immigrants.

Now, there are many instances of the official record of the name being different from the immigrant's true name. In many cases, this is due to an error on the ship's manifest. If the name was misspelled or otherwise altered on the manifest, the immigration record would reflect this incorrect name. In other cases, there was no "correct" way to spell or pronounce the name and one permissible variant was adopted as the official name.

Most of the name changes, however, were because the immigrants changed them themselves. Many anglicized their names, simplifying the spelling and pronunciation, to better fit into American society. They were Americans now and wanted to disassociate themselves with the old country. This sentiment is often difficult for us to understand today with so many Americans wanting to reconnect with their roots, but it was very common among immigrants in the late nineteenth and early twentieth centuries.

In some cases the tale may have been started by immigrant grandparents who said their family names were changed at *Ellis Island*. The term *Ellis Island* did not simply mean the processing at the immigration facility itself. It was often used to describe the entire immigration experience, including events that happened months after arrival, such as the experience of learning English, finding a new home, finding the first job in the New World, etc. Saying that the name change occurred at *Ellis Island* did not literally mean that it was changed on the day of arrival. Rather, it often meant that it was changed sometime after arrival for one reason or another.[31]

This is simply one of many linguistic legends with ethnic overtones. Others will be explored more fully in the next chapter.

chapter /ˈCHaptər/ Six

The Perils of
Political Correctness

*T*he association between words and ethnic identity is a
strong one. Not only are there myths about name chang-
ing at Ellis Island and origin stories that falsely credit words to various languages, but there is also a tendency to attribute ethnically
offensive origins to innocuous words and phrases, and the converse, to sanitize words and phrases that have offensive origins.

Sometimes a false offensive origin is simply a matter of confusion with another, similar word that is offensive. Such is the
case with *niggard*, meaning a miser. It dates to the fourteenth
century and is probably from a Scandinavian root. In contrast,
the word *nigger*, with which it is often confused, entered the
language from the French *nègre* in the late sixteenth century and
did not acquire its current spelling until the late eighteenth century.[1] Despite the radically different origins, confusion between

the two is understandable, especially in speech. The similarity of *niggard* to *nigger* in both spelling and pronunciation renders its modern use rather perilous.

Similarly, the phrase *to call a spade a spade*, meaning not to mince words or use euphemism, is the subject of similar confusion. Some believe the phrase to be racist, a use of the slang sense of *spade* meaning a black person. The phrase, however, has ancient roots, with almost two millennia of history on its modern slang cousin. English use of the phrase dates to a 1542 translation of Plutarch's *Apophthegmata* by Nicolas Udall: "Philippus aunswered, that the Macedonians wer feloes of no fyne witte in their termes but altogether grosse, clubbyshe, and rusticall, as they whiche had not the witte to calle a spade by any other name then a spade."

Plutarch, writing in 178 B.C., used the word οκαφη, meaning a basin or bowl. Erasmus, who translated Plutarch from the Greek a few years before Udall, evidently confused this word with οκαφτειον, meaning to dig. Udall, using Erasmus's book as a basis for his work, repeated the mistake. The word *spade* comes from the Old English *spadu.*²

The derogatory slang term *spade*, on the other hand, is an Americanism from the 1920s. It is a reference to the card suit, which is black, and is from a different root, the Italian *spada*, meaning sword—the symbol in the deck of cards does not represent a shovel, but is instead a stylized icon for a sword.³ Still, even with the different roots it is easy to see how confusion might arise, and those unfamiliar with Plutarch (which, let's face it, is most of us) might take offense.

But there are other offensive origin tales that truly stretch the imagination. These are not matters of simple confusion between two words that closely resemble one another. They are tortuous convolutions created to make a political point. Perhaps the most common is the origin often attributed to *picnic*.

Picnic

Popular folklore has the origin of *picnic* as coming from a name for a lynching party in the American South, a shortening of the phrase *pick a nigger*. According to the tale, whites would bring their families to the lynching and make a party out of it. The origin of this tale, like the origin of most urban legends, is unknown. This legendary origin first appears on Usenet in December 1993, but by this time the legend was already widely circulating in other media:

> I believe the word "picnic" is derived from the expression, "pick a nigger," which refers to an old practice in the American South of using lynchings as the basis for social gatherings. I saw a photograph of one of these "picnics": a bunch of dressed-up white people standing about socializing and smiling at the camera; in the background, three Black men hanging from a tree with broken necks.[4]

The story circulates widely on the internet, often accompanied by claims that the etymology is confirmed by the Smithsonian and other illustrious and credible organizations and sources. By 1998, the legend had been codified into a bit of e-mail-lore:

> This information can also be found in the African American Archives at the Smithsonian Institute. Subject: Never use the word picnic
>
> Although not taught in American learning institutions and literature, it is noted in most black history professional circles and literature, that the origin of the term "picnic" derives from the acts of lynching African Americans. The word "picnic" is rooted from the whole theme of "Pick a

Nigger." This is where white individuals would "pic" a black person to lynch and make this into a family gathering. There would be food and music and a "picnic". . . ("nic" being the white acronym for "nigger").

Scenes of this were depicted in the movie "Rosewood." We should choose to use the word "barbecue" or "outing" instead of the word picnic.

Often e-mail hoaxes like this are vectored by people who should know better. In this case, the e-mail legend as originally posted to Usenet in 1998 did not just bear the name of the Smithsonian Institution. It was allegedly from a public relations official at the Field Museum in Chicago, whose name was correctly listed along with the address and phone number of the museum on the e-mail. The official was in fact an employee of the museum in 1998. While it is possible that this was a well-executed hoax, it is more likely the museum official received the e-mail from someone and then passed it on with her name attached without questioning it or looking up *picnic* in a dictionary.[5]

Unfortunately, part of the story is true. In the late nineteenth century, the lynching of blacks was common in the South, and some of these hangings were indeed public events. However, describing them as entertainments suitable for the family is a misrepresentation. By the twentieth century, public lynchings had become unacceptable. Instead, they tended to be done by masked men in the dead of night.

As to the origin of the word *picnic*, however, the story is complete rubbish. The word *picnic* derives from the French *pique-nique*, a word that means the same thing as it does in English—an outing that includes food. *Pique* is either a reference to a leisurely style of eating (as in *pick at your food*) or to selective delicacies chosen for the outing. *Nique* is a nonsense syllable chosen to rhyme, a common pattern of word formation known as reduplication. We see similar nonsense syllables in phrases like *namby-pamby* and *itsy-bitsy*. The French word *pique-nique* appears in 1692, and *picnic* appears in English as early as 1748 in reference to picnics in Germany. The word did not gain widespread use in Britain until ca. 1800, but this is still well before the practice of lynching African Americans began in the American South.[6]

So you can enjoy your summer picnics in peace, knowing that the only racial overtone the word has is in the fevered brains of a few.

Nitty Gritty

Picnic is far from being the only term assigned unpleasant connotations by overly zealous censors. British Home Office Minister John Denham started a linguistic flap in May 2002 when he told a group of police officers that they had to "get down to the nitty gritty." Denham was told that police officers were banned from using that term because it originated as a term for the debris left at the bottom of a slave ship, after it had delivered its human cargo to the Americas.[7]

Not only is this not the origin of the term, but it turns out the British police have no list of banned words. The policy is simply to avoid using terms that could cause offense. While some police officers have complained about arbitrary application of this rule and uncertainty over what is permissible, no officers were ever disciplined for using the term *nitty gritty*.

Nitty gritty does have its origins in African-American speech, but its origin is in no way associated with slavery. The term has only been dated to 1956. Like *picnic*, it is another example of reduplication. *Nitty* is probably a nonsense word chosen to rhyme with *gritty*, although it may be a reference to *nit*, meaning a louse's egg, emphasizing uncleanliness and messiness along with *gritty*.[8]

Jimmies

Another innocent term that has been associated with false racist origins is the name for the chocolate sprinkles known as *jimmies*. For decades, children have been enjoying *jimmies* on their ice cream. The term is particularly associated with Boston and New England, but is common throughout the northeastern United States.[9] Elsewhere, they are often called *sprinkles*.

But since at least 1997, some people have associated the term *jimmies* with *Jim Crow*, or the system of laws that segregated the southern United States in the first half of the twentieth century. The following is from an October 1997 message that appeared on Usenet:

> I'd always called them sprinkles, but in Boston, the phrase "jimmies" was used to refer to chocolate-colored sprinkles, except in those establishments that reminded the patrons not to call them "jimmies" because it was racist.
>
> Whether this hints at a real etymology or a made-up one, I dunno.[10]

Later in the thread another person comments:

> I'm guessing that it may have something to do with the (presumed/folk) etymology of "Jimmies," combined with the fact that the Jimmies are generally the chocolate rather than the multicolored sprinkles. Were I a betting man, my money would be on a (presumed/folk) connection to "Jim

Crow," which was the derogatory term for black people before it became a shorthand for the Southern system of racial exclusion and disenfranchisement.[11]

Could this be the case?

The term *Jim Crow* was coined by Thomas D. Rice, ca. 1828. Rice was a minstrel performer who created a character named "Jim Crow" and gave him a characteristic song:

I'm goin, to sing a little song,
My name's Jim Crow.
Weel about and turn about and do jis so,
Eb'ry time I weel about I jump Jim Crow.

The song was quite popular and *Jim Crow* soon entered regular use to mean a black man. By 1842, *Jim Crow* was in use as an adjective designating things for blacks only. The first known adjectival use was in reference to segregated railway cars in Massachusetts in the Boston *Liberator,* January 21 of that year:

It is this spirit alone that compels the colored man to set in the "negro pew," and ride the "Jim-Crow car."[12]

This adjectival use gradually became the dominant sense of the word, and twentieth-century segregationist policies and laws came to be known as *Jim Crow*.

The term *jimmies,* meaning the ice-cream sprinkles, first appears in print in 1947,[13] but there are numerous personal attestations that the term was in use in New England as early as the 1920s. So it is chronologically plausible that chocolate *jimmies* stem from the term *Jim Crow*. But while chronology can disprove an etymology, it cannot, in and of itself, prove one.

How the name *jimmies* for the ice-cream sprinkles arose is simply not known. Various explanations have been proffered. It may be from the name of a candy maker, or it may be from *jim-jam*, a term dating from the sixteenth century that can mean a knick-knack or trivial item.

The Just Born candy company, which manufactured *jimmies* from the 1930s to the 1960s, claims that the candy was named after James Bartholomew, an employee at the company in the 1930s. Bartholomew was the employee responsible for making the chocolate sprinkles and owner Sam Born decided to name the new product after him. Just Born goes so far as to claim that they registered the word *jimmies* as a trademark. The validity of this story is questionable. While there are no documented uses of *jimmy* meaning an ice-cream sprinkle before 1947, there is anecdotal evidence to indicate the term was current in the 1920s, before Just Born began making them. Furthermore, the U.S. Patent and Trademark Office has no record of Just Born registering *jimmies* or any similar term as a trademark.[14]

Nor is there any evidence that the origin of *jimmy* is associated with Jim Crow or blacks. Many of the terms and images that we find racially insulting today were considered innocuous during the early part of the twentieth century. Advertisers were not shy about using associations that we would today consider racist and offensive. But no evidence of such associations with *jimmies* exists.

It is often said that "absence of evidence is not evidence of absence," but when one would normally expect to find evidence, its absence can be revealing. All we have to prove a racial origin for *jimmy* is the use of *jim,* and the fact that some sprinkles are chocolate. Some better evidence must be presented before one can assume a racial origin for the term.

Indian / In Dios

African Americans are not the only ethnic group that are associated with racially motivated, false etymological origins for
words and phrases. There are many others, Native Americans
for instance. Comedian George Carlin, in his 1997 book, *Brain
Droppings*, based on his stand-up routine from previous years,
comments on the etymology of the word *Indian* and whether
or not it should be considered an objectionable name for Native Americans:

> First of all, it's important to know that the word "Indian"
> does not derive from Columbus mistakenly believing he had
> reached India. India was not even called by that name in
> 1492; it was known as Hindustan. More likely, the word "In-
> dian" comes from Columbus's description of the people he
> found here. He was an Italian, and did not speak or write
> very good Spanish, so in his written accounts he called the
> Indians, "Una gente in Dios". A people in God. In God. In
> Dios. Indians. It's a perfectly noble and respectable word.[15]

Now Carlin is a very funny comedian, but he is a poor etymologist. The word *India* has been in English use since the
ninth century. It is from the Latin name for the land, which in
turn is from Greek and ultimately from the Persian *hind* and
the Sanskrit *sindhu*, meaning river, specifically the Indus
River.[16] Alexander the Great, in the third century B.C., referred
to the *Indos* River and called the inhabitants of the region *In-
dikoi*. Maps that predate Columbus's 1492 voyage label the land
Indie.

The word *Hindustan*, or more accurately *Indostan* to use the
early spelling, on the other hand, did not enter common

European use until the seventeenth century. If Columbus were to use a name for that land, it would be *India*, not Hindustan. The use of the adjective *Hindu* in European languages is even a bit later, dating to the late seventeenth century.[17]

But this myth did not originate with Carlin, although he has probably done more than anyone else to vector it. The myth is found as early as 1984 in the opening pages of Peter Matthiessen's book *Indian Country*, but even here it is simply repeating a story that has been told elsewhere:

> It has been suggested that [Columbus] named them Indios not because he imagined them to be inhabitants of India (which in the fifteenth century was still called Hindustan) but because he recognized that the friendly, generous Taino people lived in blessed harmony with their surroundings— una gente in dios, a people in God.[18]

Mattheissen is falling into an old trap and attempts to weasel out of it. He wants to use the story to illustrate a point, but he cannot find evidence that indicates that the story is true. So he uses the magical phrase *it has been suggested that* . . . With this he absolves himself of all responsibility for the truthfulness of the next statement. Whenever one encounters phrases like *it has been suggested* . . . or *it has been said* . . . warning bells should go off. What follows is very often not true. Note also that Mattheissen is more careful in his wording than Carlin is regarding the *una gente in Dios* phrase. Unlike Carlin, he does not directly state that Columbus said this. He simply allows the reader to infer it.

He does this because the phrase *una gente in Dios*, or anything like it, is found nowhere in Columbus's writings. Instead Columbus simply refers to the lands he found as *las Indias* and to their inhabitants as *los Indios*. It is clear from his writings that Columbus thought he had arrived in Asia and that the people he encountered were Asians:

> On the thirty-third day after I departed from Cadiz, I came to the Indian sea, where I found many islands inhabited by men without number, of all which I took possession for our most fortunate king, with proclaiming heralds and flying standards, no one objecting. To the first of these I gave the name of the blessed Saviour, on whose aid relying I had reached this as well as the other islands. But the Indians call it Guanahany. I also called each one of the others by a new name. For I ordered one island to be called Santa Maria of the Conception, another Fernandina, another Isabella, another Juana, and so on with the rest.[19]

So the facts behind this myth are false, but what about its "lesson"? Is the word *Indian* offensive when applied to Native Americans? First, no name is inherently offensive. Names like this begin life as simple descriptions. In this case, the description is inaccurate, but Columbus did not use the term in an offensive manner. Over time, the use of such names in pejorative contexts can give the word offensive connotations and render the word unacceptable. Such is the case with the word *nigger*, which originally simply meant black. Centuries of use in pejorative contexts have rendered that word taboo. The term *Indian* has not reached that point. Some consider it to be offensive preferring the term *Native American*; others do not.

The *Indian/In Dios* myth is an example of what linguists refer to as the etymological fallacy. This is the belief that the original meaning of a word is the "true" meaning. By fabricating and repeating a story that imbues the term with a noble origin, people like Mattheissen and Carlin are trying to reclaim the word for acceptable speech. But the problem is that the origin of a word does not determine its meaning. A word's meaning comes from usage, not etymology. If people continue to use *Indian* in pejorative contexts it will become an insult. If it is used in positive or neutral contexts, it will be, respectively, a positive or neutral term.

Indian Giver

The creation of euphemistic origins for Native American terms is not restricted to the word *Indian*. Another example is the term *Indian giver*. The term, as commonly used today, means someone who gives a gift only to later demand its return.

The myth is that the term *Indian giver* does not refer to Native Americans who give gifts and then demand their return, but rather that it comes from those who give gifts to Native Americans only to take them away later, in other words, white men. The term, according to the myth, does not cast aspersions on Native Americans; rather it echoes the broken promises the whites made to the Indians.

The key to understanding the origin is not to look at how we use the term today, but rather to look at how it was used when it was first coined. The noun *Indian gift* dates to 1765 when Thomas Hutchinson records the following in *The history of the Province of Massachusetts Bay*: "An Indian gift is a proverbial expression, signifying a present for which an equivalent return is expected."

The term *Indian giver* first appears a century later in Bartlett's 1860 *Dictionary of Americanisms*: "When an Indian gives any thing, he expects to receive an equivalent, or to have his gift returned."

By the 1890s, the sense had shifted to mean one who demands a gift be returned and had become a playground word among children. The following is from the *Journal of American Folklore*, 1892:

> If an American child, who has made a small gift to a play-mate is indiscreet enough to ask that the gift be returned, he (or she) is immediately accused of being an Indian-giver, or, as it is commonly pronounced Injun-giver.[20]

The origin of the term is rooted in different commercial practices, and the pejorative connotations of the term are based on a cultural misunderstanding. To the Native Americans, who had no concept of money or currency, gifts were a form of trade, goods that were bartered and exchanged. One did not give a gift without expecting one of equivalent value in return. If one could not offer an equivalent return gift, the original gift would be refused or returned. To Europeans, with their mone-tary-based trade practices, this seemed low and insulting. Gifts were not for trade, but were to be freely given.

Unlike *Indian*, the term *Indian-giver* is unequivocally pejo-rative. But it stems not from the dishonesty of either white men or Native Americans, but rather from a European misun-derstanding of Native American cultural and trade practices. Europeans were using the standards of their own culture to evaluate those of Native Americans, and in that light the de-manding of a return gift was certainly distasteful and insulting. But in terms of Native American culture, it was no more in-sulting to ask for a return gift than it would be to ask for pay-ment for a purchase in a white man's store.

So far we have seen two distinct patterns in politically cor-rect etymological myth. One pattern is to assign a false pejora-tive origin, as in *picnic*, *nitty gritty*, and *jimmy*. The second is to assign a false euphemistic origin, as in *Indian* or *Indian giver*. The difference has nothing to do with the ethnic groups in question. It is certainly possible, for example, to have pejorative origins falsely assigned to Native American terms. The word *squaw* is one such case.

Squaw

Squaw is borrowed from the Narragansett word for woman and has cognates in other Algonquin languages. It appears in English in 1634, shortly after the first European settlements in New England.[21] But this is not the origin that popular myth would give it. Instead, the myth is that *squaw* is a Native American word meaning either prostitute or vagina.

Is *squaw* pejorative? That depends on the context. Certainly the term has been used with disdain. Whites did not hold Native American marriage practices in high regard, so the term was often used by English-speakers to mean a mistress or prostitute. And addressing a Native American woman as *squaw* could be considered offensive in the same way that addressing a Caucasian female as *woman* is offensive.

It is also worthwhile pointing out that *squaw* is a Narragansett word and would not be a native term in most other Native American tongues. So to call a non-Algonquin woman *squaw* is akin to calling a Frenchwoman *Frau*.

This last is complicated by the use of pidgins by Native Americans and leads us into a general misunderstanding about Native American languages. In popular culture, movies, western novels, and the like, Indians are often depicted as speaking a broken, ungrammatical English, studded with words like *heap* (big), *papoose* (baby), and *squaw* (woman). The Lone Ranger's "faithful Indian companion" Tonto is our cultural template for how we perceive Native American languages.

Many today perceive this depiction of Native American speech to be insulting, pointing out that Native American languages possess large vocabularies and complex grammatical rules and structures. They are every bit as complex and grammatical as English (see "500 Eskimo Words for Snow" in chapter 1, p. 50). This is true, but it also only part of the story.

Native Americans often did actually speak the "broken" English depicted in popular movies and books, but this is not a representation of Native American language. Rather, it is a representation of a pidgin used by Indians to communicate with whites and with members of other tribes.

When the Europeans first arrived in North America there were over 300 Native American languages spoken on the continent. Many of these were as unrelated to one another as French is to Vietnamese. As the whites moved west and forcibly resettled Native Americans in new lands, the Indians encountered tribes and languages that they had never seen or heard before. There was need to communicate.

A pidgin is a simple contact language, used for trade and other basic communication purposes. Native Americans adopted a pidgin, or "broken," English to speak with whites and with those in other tribes. The vocabulary of this language was pretty much universal across the continent, consisting mainly of English words, but with some Native American (like *squaw*), French, and Spanish words thrown in for good measure. The grammar, like that of all pidgins, is radically simplified. Most inflections have been lost in favor of a few, universal endings. The suffix –*um*, for example, is used for most transitive verb forms, as in *makum* (to make something) or *paddlum* (to paddle something, like a canoe).[22]

Here is an actual sample of this pidgin (taken from life, not literature) from a Native American woman proposing to a white man:

You silly. You weak. You baby-hands. No catch horse. No
kill buffalo. No good, but for sit still—read book. Never
mind. Me like. Me make rich. Me make big man. Me your
squaw.

Or here is a sample of an Ogallala Sioux chief speaking: "Good
Indian me. Heap good Indian, hunt buffalo and deer."[23]

Note that in both these cases, the Indian is speaking pidgin
to a white person, who presumably does not speak the relevant
Native American tongue. The Ogallala Sioux chief would not
talk in this simple fashion to his own people, but only to outsiders who did not speak his native language.

So are depictions of this pidgin in popular literature accurate? Yes, they are. But the issue is what they depict. As depictions of a pidgin used by Native Americans they are accurate.
They are nothing like the true Native American languages.

Hip / Hep

How many times have we given a hearty *Hip! Hip! Hurrah!* in
congratulations for some deed or feat? Every time we said this,
were we repeating an anti-Semitic slur? The legend would have
it so. The 1898 edition of Brewer's *Dictionary of Phrase and Fable* says the following:

Hip! Hip! Hurrah!
   Hip is said to be a notarica, composed of the initial letters
of Hierosolyma Est Per'dita. Henri van Laun says, in Notes
and Queries, that whenever the German knights headed a
Jew-hunt in the Middle Ages, they ran shouting "Hip! Hip!"
as much as to say "Jerusalem is destroyed."

Timbs derives Hurrah from the Sclavonic hù-raj (to Paradise), so that Hip! hip! hurrah! would mean "Jerusalem is lost to the infidel, and we are on the road to Paradise." These etymons may be taken for what they are worth. The word hurrah! is a German exclamation also.[24]

A careful reading of Brewer's words makes it clear that he does not believe this etymology, even though he is often cited as evidence of this origin. There is, however, a germ of truth to this legend.

Some trace the origin of *hep* to the sacking of the Jerusalem by the Romans in A.D. 135. Others claim it dates to the Crusades. But despite these claims, no solid evidence of cries of *Hep!* or the phrase *Hierosolyma Est Perdita* can be found dating them to either Roman or Medieval times. Instead, this particular phrase and the cry of *Hep!* in reference to a pogrom date only to the early nineteenth century.

In 1819 there were anti-Semitic riots in Germany and elsewhere in Europe. In Würzburg, students in the riots did chant "Hep! Hep!" and the riots of that year came to be called the Hep Hep Riots. The question is what did the students mean by *hep*? It is possible they were shouting an abbreviation of a Latin phrase or they could have been using a goatherd's cry. Nineteenth-century German goatherds would shout *Hep!* to drive the goats along. The students could have been imitating this.

Regardless of what the students of Würzburg meant by their shouts, it is not the origin of *hip* in *Hip! Hip! Hurrah!* English use of the cheer predates the 1819 riots. Use of *hip* as an exclamation or a call dates to mid-eighteenth century. Thomas Moore's *Memoirs* has the following from 1818, a year before the riots: "They hipped and hurraed me."[25] *Hurrah* is even older than *hip*, dating to the late seventeenth century.[26]

So there is a grain of truth to the legend in that the cry of *Hep!* has been associated with anti-Semitism since the early nineteenth century, but the main point of the legend is false. The cheer of *Hip! Hip! Hurrah!* is etymologically unconnected to the anti-Semitic cry.

Gay

Ethnic groups are not the only ones who have myths about the words used to label them. Any group that suffers social opprobrium is likely to develop origin myths about their labels. The socially preferred term for homosexuals, especially homosexual men although it applies to lesbians as well, is *gay*. There are several myths and misperceptions circulating regarding this word.

The first of these is that *gay* began life as an acronym. It is sometimes said to stem from the phrase *good as you*, a call for equality. It is also sometimes given the much more politically incorrect meaning of *Got AIDS Yet?* This last, fortunately, does not seem to have much currency as a belief; most people accept it for what it is, a very offensive joke.

A more common belief is that *gay* acquired the homosexual sense rather recently, in the late 1960s with the Stonewall riot and the rise of the gay rights movement. This is not the case. The American public became aware of this sense of the word in the late 1960s and early 1970s, but the term is in fact much older, being used by homosexuals as a term of self-reference as early as the 1920s, or perhaps even earlier.

The earliest citation of the homosexual sense of *gay* in the *Historical Dictionary of American Slang* is a 1922 quotation from Gertrude Stein's "Miss Furr & Mrs. Skeene," which appeared in the magazine *Vanity Fair*. It is uncertain, however, if Stein's use of gay in this case is a reference to lesbians or to the [then] conventional sense of *gay* meaning happy: "They were . . . gay, they learned little things that are things in being gay, . . . they were quite regularly gay."[27]

The first unequivocal written use of *gay* to mean homosexual is from 1929, in Noel Coward's musical *Bittersweet*. In the song "Green Carnation," four overdressed, 1890s dandies sing:

Pretty boys, witty boys, You may sneer
At our disintegration.
Haughty boys, naughty boys,
Dear, dear, dear!
Swooning with affectation . . .
And as we are the reason
For the "Nineties" being gay,
We all wear a green carnation.

The penultimate line refers to the 1890s, which were commonly called the *gay nineties*. In general usage, the term *gay nineties* has nothing to do with homosexuality, but in this context Coward clearly intends it as a double entendre.

Gay appears in several 1930s movies as a double entendre or a code word intended to slip past the Hays Commission censors. The most famous use of *gay* in a picture of that era is in the 1938 comedy classic *Bringing Up Baby*, starring Cary Grant and Katharine Hepburn. In one scene Grant appears in drag. When asked why he is wearing women's clothing he replies: "Because I just went gay all of a sudden."[28]

So, *gay* is known to have appeared by 1929 and was well established as a slang or jargon term by the 1930s. But could the term be even older? There is at least one claim that it is. But like the Stein quotation above, this earlier use is of uncertain

meaning and could simply be a use of the traditional sense of
gay meaning happy.

The word appears in an 1868 song by female impersonator
Will S. Hays titled, "Gay Young Clerk in the Dry Goods
Store." The lyrics do not explicitly link the word with homosexuality, but they can be interpreted that way, especially if
sung by a man in drag. Then again, that may be reading too
much into the lyrics. Given the gap in years between this song
and the first unequivocal use of *gay* to mean homosexual in
1929, it is probable that its use in the lyrics simply means
happy. But since it is a question of interpretation, here are the
lyrics in question. You can judge for yourself:

> It's about a chap, perhaps you know,
> I'm told he is "Nobody's beau,"
> But maybe you all knew that before,
> He's a lively clerk in a Dry-Goods Store.
> O! Augustus Dolphus is his name,
> From Skiddy-ma-dink they say he came,
> He's a handsome man and he's proud and poor,
> This gay young clerk in the Dry-Goods Store.

OK, we've established, with some certainty, when *gay* came
into use, but how did the word come to be associated with homosexuality? Several possibilities exist.

The most likely explanation is that it is a clipping of *gaycat*
or *geycat*, a slang term for a tramp or hobo who is young and
new to life on the road. *Gaycats* were commonly in the company of older tramps, with the implication of a homosexual relationship. Gaycats were often employed as lookouts while
their older partner committed crimes. The term is of unknown
origin but dates to at least 1893.[29]

Another possible origin is in the nineteenth-century slang use of *gay* as a euphemism for prostitution. This slang sense grew out of the general sense of *gay* meaning addicted to social pleasures. The general sense dates to the seventeenth century, but the more specialized prostitution sense first appears in Davis's *Post-Captain* from 1805:

> As our heroes passed along the Strand, they were accosted by a hundred gay ladies, who asked them if they were good-natured. "Devil take me! . . . there is not a girl in the Strand that I would touch with my gloves on."[30]

This sexual sense of the term could have become associated with homosexual promiscuity and the heterosexual sense lost.

The hobo and the prostitution theories are not mutually exclusive. They both could have influenced and shaped the rise of the contemporary sense of *gay*.

Faggot

A more derogatory term, but no less interesting in the folklore department, is *faggot* and its clipped form *fag*. The primary legend regarding the origin of *faggot* is that the term dates to the Middle Ages and is a reference to burning homosexuals at the stake, the *faggot* being the wood used to stoke the fire. Over time the term transferred to the victim. The legend, like the similar one surrounding *picnic*, is false.

Like many linguistic legends, this one has elements of truth. The sense of *faggot* meaning a bundle of sticks does indeed date to medieval times, although the homosexual sense does not. *Faggot*, in the sense of a bundle of firewood, is first recorded ca. 1300 and by the sixteenth century had acquired the meaning of an execution by being burnt alive. Phrases like *fire and faggot* and *fry a faggot* were used in reference to executions. These terms did not, however, have any connotations linking them with homosexuality. They could just as easily be applied to heretics, witches, and common criminals.

It was not until twentieth-century America that *faggot* acquired the sense of homosexuality. This sense appears in 1914, first recorded in Jackson and Hellyer's *A Vocabulary of Criminal Slang*: "All the fagots (sissies) will be dressed in drag at the ball tonight."

So how did a word meaning a bundle of sticks come to be a derogatory term for a gay man? The key is in another sense of the word.

Since the late sixteenth century, 1591 to be exact, *faggot* has been used to mean an old or bad-tempered woman, a shrew or battleaxe.[31] A bundle of sticks was a burden, and a man would use the term to refer to his wife just as a modern husband might say *the old ball and chain.*

The term attached to gay men because of their perceived effeminate qualities. *Faggot* lost the shrewish, burdensome qualities, and instead the feminine qualities were emphasized. In this way it is similar to *queen* or *fairy*. Any connection to the firewood used for executions is pure fancy.

Another common legend refers to the practice, in English public schools, of junior students performing drudgework for their seniors. *To fag* is to perform such work, and the junior students are referred to as *fags*. Many assume that this, and the implication of a homosexual relationship between the students, is the origin. In fact, this sense of *fag* is etymologically unrelated. The verb dates to the sixteenth century and is probably an alteration of *to flag*, meaning to tire.[32]

Another version is that the word comes from the British use of *fag*—a cigarette. This is often accompanied with a complex explanation that the way one holds a cigarette is a surreptitious signal of one's homosexuality. Again, this cigarette sense is etymologically unrelated. It is a clipping of *fag-end*, from an obsolete sense of *fag*, meaning something that hangs loose.[33]

Handicap

Handicapped persons are another non-ethnic group that suffer social dislocation and have a false origin story associated with their name. There is a false belief that *handicapped*, meaning disabled, derives from begging, or literally from *hand in cap*. *Handicapped* people, so the legend goes, could only make a living by begging, holding out their hats or caps for people to place their money in. The word does have its origins with hands in caps, but it has nothing to do with begging and originally does not refer to disability at all.

Instead, *handicap* comes from an old method of setting the odds for a wager. Two bettors would engage a neutral umpire to determine the odds in an unequal contest. The bettors would put their hands holding forfeit money into a hat or cap. The umpire would announce the odds and the bettors would withdraw their hands—hands full if they accepted the odds and the bet was on, hands empty if they did not accept the bet and were willing to forfeit the money. If one bettor forfeited, the money went to the other bettor. If both agreed on either forfeiting or going ahead with the wager, the umpire kept the money as payment.

This method of setting odds dates to at least 1362 when it was described in *Piers Plowman*:

"Clement þe cobelere caste of his cloke", for which "Hikke þe hakeneyman" wagered his hood, and "Robyn þe ropere" was named for "a noumpere", to ordain how much "who-so haueth the hood shuld haue amendes of the cloke".

The term *handicap* appears ca. 1653 in George Daniel's *Idyllia*: "Ev'n those who now command, The inexorable Roman, were but what One step had given: Handy-Capps in Fate." The word is used in its modern sense about a century later in *Pond's Racing Calendar* of 1754:

> Rules concerning Racing in general, with a Description of a Post and Handy-Cap Match. . . . A Handy-Cap Match, if for A. B. and C. to put an equal Sum into a Hat, C, which is the HandyCapper, makes a Match for A. and B. which when perused by them, they put their Hands into their Pockets and draw them out closed, then they open them together, and if both have Money in their Hands, the Match is confirm'd; if neither have Money, it is no Match: In both Cases the Hand-Capper draws all the Money out of the Hat; but if one has Money in his Hand, and the other none, then it is no Match; and he that has the Money in his Hand is intitled to the Deposit in the Hat. If a Match is made without the Weight being mentioned, each Horse must carry ten Stone.

The sense meaning disabled comes from the horseracing term, in which the umpire decrees the superior horse should carry extra weight—a handicap. A disabled person also carries an extra burden. The sense of *handicapped* denoting a disabled person appears around 1915.[34]

Not all of these euphemistic and dysphemistic origin stories are related to particularly ethnic and social groups. The term *politically correct* itself has a politically correct origin myth associated with it.

Politically Correct

There is a myth that the term and concept of *politically correct* were invented in the 1990s by conservatives who wished to lambaste liberals:

> The term "political correctness" was coined in the early 1990s, in the midst of a controversy over perceived threats to academic freedom on America's college and university campuses. Originally an approving phrase used by those on the Leninist Left to denote someone who steadfastly toed the party line, "politically correct" or "P. C." was later used ironically by critics of the Left—first by conservatives such as Dinesh D'Souza and then by many old-school liberals who sought to defend campus freedoms against "P. C." censors.[35]

The term and the concept are actually considerably older and were never particularly associated with Leninism, at least not in English usage. It is true that conservative critics have used some of the excesses of the Left to lampoon and criticize liberals; and those critics have conflated various different liberal ideas under a single rubric of *political correctness*, but they did not coin the term nor imagine the movement.

The first known use of *politically correct* dates all the way back to 1793. It appears in a legal opinion written by Justice James Wilson in *Chisholm v. Georgia*:

> The states, rather than the people, for whose sake the states exist, are frequently the objects which attract and arrest our principal attention. . . . Sentiments and expressions of this inaccurate kind prevail in our common, even in our convivial, language. . . . "The United States", instead of the "People of the United States", is the toast given. This is not politically correct.

It appears again in 1936 in H.V. Morton's *In the Steps of Saint Paul*:

> It has often been asked why Paul addressed his converts as "Galatians". But is there any other word that could have described so mixed a crowd? . . . "Galatians", a term that was politically correct, embraced everyone under Roman rule.

These early uses, however, do not embrace the term as we do today. In these cases, the term meant appropriate to the particular political context and circumstances. As late as 1979, the term was still being used in this older, nonspecific sense, as in an *Economist* article from January 6 of that year: "His judgement that the time and place called for an attack on the quality and efficiency of the municipal government proved to be politically correct."

But by 1970, *politically correct* was also being used in a very different sense, meaning conforming to a particular set of Leftist views that rejected non-conforming speech and behavior. The first known use of this more specific sense is in Toni Cade's *Black Woman* (1970): "A man cannot be politically correct and a chauvinist too."

Other early uses of *politically correct* include a 1975 statement by the president of the National Organization for Women, Karen DeCrow: "On the lesbian issue, she said NOW was moving in the 'intellectually and politically correct direction.'" In 1984, it was the Women's Studies International Forum that used the term:

> The deformed sexuality of patriarchal culture must be moved . . . into an arena for struggle, where a "politically correct" sexuality of mutual respect will contend with an "incorrect" sexuality of domination and submission.

And in 1991, the *Village Voice* picked up the term: "I've been chided by a reader for using the word gringos and informed that European American is politically correct."

The converse of *politically incorrect* first appeared in 1947, in Nabokov's *Bend Sinister*, but Nabokov used it as the converse of the original sense:

A person who has never belonged to a Masonic Lodge or to a fraternity, club, union, or the like, is an abnormal and dangerous person. . . . It is better for a man to have belonged to a politically incorrect organization than not to have belonged to any organization at all.

In 1977, the *Washington Post* used *politically incorrect* as the converse of the second, more specific sense: "The African Liberation Day Coalition explained that both the other groups held politically incorrect positions."[36]

The abbreviation *PC* first appears in 1986.[37] And by 1992, the *political correctness* movement was coming in for criticism and parody. However, this criticism did not originate with conservatives, but rather with more centrist members of the Left wing. That year attendees at the Democratic National Convention were given a humorous pamphlet titled *The Official Politically Correct Dictionary and Handbook*. The pamphlet, among other things, defined ballot-box stuffing as "nontraditional voting," and sore loser as an "equanimity-deprived individual with temporarily unmet career objectives."[38]

The idea that *politically correct* stems from Marxist-Leninist thought does have some merit. Mao Zedong—in a 1963 essay called *Where Do Correct Ideas Come From?*—discusses "thinking correctly." Mao outlined the theory that people can be led to accept political ideas through language usage. But whether this essay, which was not translated into English and published in the West until 1968, had an impact on American Leftist thought quickly enough to generate the theory of and phrase *political correctness* is questionable.[39]

Everyday words can also be assigned euphemistic origin myths. In chapter 4, p. 106, we examined the myth of *cold enough to freeze the balls off a brass monkey*—an example of a somewhat blue term that is rendered more palatable by a euphemistic origin. It is not the only such phrase.

Tinker's Damn

Not worth a tinker's damn is an often-uttered phrase, although many people nowadays have no idea what a tinker is. There is also considerable confusion over the word *damn* in this phrase, which is often bowdlerized as *dam*.

A *tinker* is an itinerant tradesman who mends pots and pans. The name could derive from either the sound of a bell that the tinker rang to announce he was in the neighborhood (perhaps the name Tinkerbell from James Barrie's *Peter Pan* is an allusion to this practice), or it could be an onomatopoeic phrase for the tinking sound the tradesman made as he worked on the pots and pans. This second explanation appears first in 1440, and Samuel Johnson, in his 1755 dictionary, agrees with it.

Many etymologists side with Dr. Johnson, but there are also those who disagree. The earliest citation in the *OED*2 dates from 1265 and is a surname: *Editha le Tynekere*. This is of interest because it refers to a tradeswoman, not a man. Other sources date the surname *Tynker* as early as 1252, and the Scottish form, *tinkler*, to 1175.[40]

The verb to *tink*, meaning to mend a pot, dates only to the fifteenth century, and the words *tink* and *tinkle*, referring to the bell or metallic sound, date only to Wyclif's 1382 translation of the Bible, 1 Cor 13:1: "I am maad as bras sownnynge or a symbal tynkynge."[41] Presumably the verb would have come before the noun, but earlier uses of the verb may just be unrecorded or the verb could be a back-formation from the noun. It is very possible, and perhaps probable, that *tinker* comes from the word *tin*, the material with which the tinker worked.

But what about *damn*? Some say that it should be spelled *dam* because it is not a curse, but rather a term for a method used in mending pots. The most common folkloric explanation appears in 1877 in Edward Knight's *The Practical Dictionary of Mechanics*: "Tinker's-dam, a wall of dough raised around a place which a plumber desires to flood with a coat of solder. The material can be but once used; being consequently thrown away as worthless, it has passed into a proverb, usually involving the wrong spelling of the otherwise innocent word 'dam.'"

This explanation just does not wash. First, there is no record of the spelling *tinker's dam* until Knight penned the above explanation. The phrase also appears in 1824 as *tinker's curse* in John MacTaggart's *The Scottish Gallovidian Encyclopedia*: "A tinkler's curse she did na care What she did think or say."

Henry David Thoreau, in 1839, was the first to use the form *tinker's damn*. *Dam* is clearly a Victorian bowdlerization, and Knight's explanation is an attempt to justify it. Similarly, others have suggested that the *dam* is a reference to the tinker's horse, usually a worthless nag. This explanation not only shares the problem of chronology with Knight's explanation, but *dam* does not mean horse; it means mother. A horse has a sire and a dam—a father and a mother.

The origin of the phrase is most likely the simplest explanation. Tinkers had a reputation for cursing, and a *tinker's damn* was not worth much because tinkers damned everything—supply and demand.

Legends are not always about those on the bottom rungs of the social ladder, whether they be Blacks, Native Americans, the disabled, or lower-class tradesmen. Sometimes legends afflict the high and mighty, as we shall see in the next chapter.

Wax Tadpoles and Jelly Doughnuts

O ne class of linguistic urban legends are alleged mistranslations that result in humorous consequences. Often the
point of these stories is to deflate the rich and powerful. A
politician or corporate executive makes a mistake that humbles
them. There is also a bit of a xenophobic bent to these legends,
conveying the message that dealing with other cultures is
fraught with peril.

Most of these legends are based on an incomplete understanding of the other language involved. There is a grain of
truth at the core, enough to make the legend sound plausible
to someone recalling their high school Spanish or German, but
overall the legend is false.

I Am a Jelly Doughnut

Presidential language gaffes are nothing new. In recent years, George W. Bush and former Vice President Dan Quayle have been lambasted for errors in their speech and spelling. Some of this criticism is deserved, some of it not. And as we have seen with the history of *OK*, this tradition of criticizing a politician's command of the language goes back at least as far as Andrew Jackson.

Occasionally, a president or other politician will say something that is translated poorly. In one famous incident in Warsaw, Poland, in December 1977, a State Department translator for Jimmy Carter made several such gaffes in a single speech. When Carter said, "when I left the United States," the interpreter translated it as "when I abandoned the United States." When the president spoke of the desires of the Polish people, it was translated as "your lusts for the future." These and other mistakes brought laughter from the crowd.

Part of the problem was that the interpreter was speaking in rustic dialect of Polish, using, as one Polish journalist put it, "antiquated words and strange grammar just like uneducated Polish peasants still do." The American-born interpreter probably learned his Polish from a family member who was from a provincial region of Poland. The interpreter also evidently inserted some Russian words into the translation, and confused Russian and Polish words with one another on several occasions.[1]

Sometimes a president will attempt to say something in a foreign language. Fortunately, other than odd pronunciation, no president has ever embarrassed himself by making a misstep in a foreign tongue—they are too well prepped in delivering these scripted nuggets. But there is one urban legend about a president who allegedly did. It was John F. Kennedy and the year was 1963. In a speech at the newly erected Berlin Wall,

Kennedy said: "Two thousand years ago the proudest boast was 'civis Romanus sum.' Today, in the world of freedom, the proudest boast is 'Ich bin ein Berliner.' [. . .] All free men, wherever they may live, are citizens of Berlin, and, therefore, as a free man, I take pride in the words 'Ich bin ein Berliner.' "[2] It is inspiring stuff. But according to the legend, what Kennedy said in German translates as *I am a jelly-filled pastry*.

The noun *Berliner* has two meanings in German. It can mean a male native of Berlin or it can mean a jelly-filled pastry (much like *Hamburger* can mean someone from Hamburg or ground beef). In the standard German dialect, when one declares where one comes from, the indefinite article is usually omitted. In German, a man from Berlin would normally say, *Ich bin Berliner*.

The legend insists that if you include the indefinite article, you are not referring to a native of Berlin, but rather to the pastry. If you want to say *I am a pastry*, you include the indefinite article. Thus to be grammatically correct, Kennedy should have said, *Ich bin Berliner*. This is where the legend goes wrong.

It is not ungrammatical in German to say, *Ich bin ein Berliner*. In fact Kennedy's use of the *ein* is a very precise and grammatically correct statement. A native of Berlin would omit the *ein*, but when speaking metaphorically a non-native includes the indefinite article. Kennedy was not literally claiming that he was from Berlin, but rather that he was to be counted among the people of Berlin. Had Kennedy omitted the *ein*, he would not have been making a metaphorical statement that he stood alongside the people of Berlin in their struggle against communism. Instead he would have been making a false statement claiming Berlin as the place of his residence or birth.

Robert Lochner, Kennedy's translator for the trip, provided the line in Kennedy's speech. Lochner, who had grown up in

Berlin and attended German schools there, was completely familiar with the Berlin dialect. Prior to giving the speech, Kennedy practiced the lines with Berlin Mayor (and later chancellor of West Germany) Willy Brandt, who found no fault with the translation.

Furthermore, some German dialects use the indefinite article when making statements about where one is from. While this is not typically done in the Berlin dialect, it is common in Bavaria, Austria, and Switzerland. So, while a Berliner might not use the indefinite article, Kennedy's grammatical construction was hardly unusual to the German ear. When a Bavarian says, "Ich bin ein Bayer," no one mistakes him for an aspirin.

Finally, people from Berlin do not refer to the pastries as *Berliners*. Rather, they call them *Pfannkuchen*. It is only in the Rhine River region and in Switzerland that the pastries are known as *Berliners*.[3]

So, no one in the audience that day thought Kennedy was speaking about pastries. No one laughed. Instead, they cheered the line. After the fact, some German comedians made a joke of it, which likely started the legend.

Chevy No Go

Presidents and politicians are not the only ones to commit gaffes in translation. Legend would have marketing departments of major corporations do so as well. The reason for the popularity of such tales is much the same as those about presidential gaffes. These legends make fun of the rich and powerful, and they feed our xenophobia by warning against the dangers and pitfalls of foreign trade.

But when we move into the realm of legends about international marketing blunders, another factor comes into play— that of international business consultants and firms that provide translation and localization services. Such firms promote tales of corporate misadventures in the realm of international business because it makes their services seem all the more valuable. One of the most pervasive of these business legends is that of the Chevrolet Nova and its Latin American sales. Here is the legend as told by one international business "expert":

> "General Motors . . . was troubled by the lack of enthusiasm among the Puerto Rican auto dealers for its recently introduced Chevrolet Nova. The word nova means 'star' when translated literally. However, when spoken, it sounds like 'no va,' which in Spanish means 'it does not go.' This obviously did little to increase consumer confidence in the new vehicle. To remedy the situation, General Motors changed the automobile name to Caribe and sales increased."[4]

There are many variations in this tale, in which the country where the Nova allegedly failed to sell changes. Here it is Puerto Rico. Most commonly it is Mexico. Other times another Spanish-speaking country is given.

The tale is one of the pitfalls of not doing market research and presumably of not hiring high-priced business consultants to conduct that research. Well, General Motors was wise not to hire the consultants who vector this legend. The irony is that it is not General Motors who failed to do their research, but the consultants who tell this legend.

The most easily debunked aspect of the story is the bit about renaming the Nova to Caribe. There is a car marketed as Caribe in Latin America, but Volkswagen makes it, not General Motors. The Caribe is the same car that is marketed in the United States under the names Rabbit and Golf.

International sales figures for individual car models are more difficult to track down, and generally not available to the public.

However, urban legend researcher David Mikkelson managed to get a response from General Motors' marketing department in 1993.

The company told him that General Motors introduced the Chevrolet Nova into the U.S. market in 1962. It sold very well and in 1972, the company decided to introduce it into the Latin American market, in particular into Mexico and Venezuela. It sold well in both countries under the *Nova* name. General Motors described the sales as "very strong, surpassing initial expectations."[5]

While *no va* does indeed mean "no go," Spanish also has the word *nova*, which like the English word, comes from the Latin for new. The Spanish *nova* is spelled as one word, not two, and it is pronounced differently from *no va*, with the accent on the first syllable, instead of the second. Like Germans and *Berliner*, Spanish speakers would not confuse the two. An English-language equivalent would be someone believing that the word *carpet* refers to animal that one keeps in an automobile. Just as no English speaker would ever be confused by *carpet*, no Spanish speaker would be confused by *nova*.

Furthermore, Pemex, the Mexican government-owned oil company, sells a brand of gasoline under the name *Nova*. So when the Chevy *Nova* was introduced, there was even a connection between the car and a popular brand of gas. No, the General Motors executives were not a bunch of clueless gringos. They had done their market research (something promulgators of urban legends would be wise to do more of) and concluded that *Nova* was an appropriate name for the market. They were right.

Bite the Wax Tadpole

General Motors is not the only company to have an urban legend about its foreign marketing practices. Another famous one is about Coca-Cola in China.

The legend says that the name *Coca-Cola* in Chinese means *bite the wax tadpole*. When Coca-Cola initially tried to market to China, their sales were terrible. Just as no Mexican would buy a car that did not run, no Chinese would want to eat tadpoles, wax or otherwise. Unlike the Chevy Nova story, there is a grain of truth in this legend, but just a grain.

Coca-Cola was introduced into the Chinese market in 1928. The marketing department of Coca-Cola (which is acknowledged as one of the best in the world—look where it has gotten them) took great care in making sure the name of their product was translated in a way that both represented the appropriate pronunciation as well as connoted a favorable product image. This was not an easy task.

Written Chinese has some 40,000 characters. Of these, about 200 can be used to form a name in the Mandarin dialect that could be pronounced like *Coca-Cola* is in English. The problem for the soft drink manufacturer was that most of these combinations produced strings of nonsense words. The marketers were primarily interested in coming up with a Chinese name with the proper pronunciation, but they were also concerned that the meaning of name could not be turned into a joke. While the marketers wrestled with this problem, the first shipments of Coke reached Chinese shores.

Some Chinese shopkeepers created hand-lettered signs advertising the new soda. The characters used in these signs could be pronounced as *Coca-Cola*, but could mean a variety of nonsensical things. One of the combinations could be translated as *bite the wax tadpole*. Another translated as *mare fastened with wax*. Later that year, the Coca-Cola marketing department settled on a combination of four characters with the appropriate pronunciation, and which could be translated as "let the mouth rejoice."[6]

So yes, there is a combination of characters in Mandarin that sounds like *Coca-Cola* and means *bite the wax tadpole*. But the Coca-Cola Company never used that combination in its marketing efforts, and the few hand-lettered signs that did use them did not materially affect sales of the soda. The Coca-Cola marketing department was not negligent and did not err in translating the name of their product. The truth is the opposite. Coca-Cola took great care that the translation was both accurate and meaningful.

Coke's main competitor is not let off the hook by linguistic legends either. Pepsi also allegedly had similar problems in China. Only this time, Pepsi's slogan *Come alive with Pepsi!* is translated into Chinese as *Pepsi brings your dead ancestors back to life.*

No one has been able to pin this legend down. For one thing, the English-language version of the slogan, in use starting in 1963, is *Come alive! You're in the Pepsi generation,* so the form of the legend most frequently encountered does not even get the English slogan right. Further, the legend does not specify the dialect of Chinese into which it is translated. Most Chinese dialects use the same character set and the written forms are mutually intelligible, but the pronunciations and spoken forms can vary widely. Complicating the situation is that sometimes other countries, usually Thailand, are cited as the locale for the legend.

While we cannot say for certain, the Pepsi story is probably untrue. It seems likely that it is a variant of the Coke *bite the wax tadpole* story. Only here, instead of the locale changing, it is the brand of soda.

There are dozens of infamous mistranslation-of-advertisement stories. Most cannot be either verified or definitively refuted. The problem is the loss of critical details and variations in the telling. Most of the time, critical details like dates and the actual wording of the foreign translation are omitted. Because of these variations and omissions, it is usually impossible to verify whether the ad campaign in question even existed, much less whether there was a translation error in it.

Turn It Loose and Fly Naked

A good example of a mistranslation-of-advertisement legend is that the Coors brewing company translated its slogan *Turn It Loose* into a Spanish phrase that could mean to suffer from diarrhea. In this case, the common versions of the legend include the Spanish wording (a rarity in such legends). Depending on which version of the story you believe, the slogan was either translated as "suéltalo con Coors" (let it go loose with Coors) or "suéltate con Coors" (set yourself free with Coors). The legend says that these literal translations mean diarrhea in colloquial Spanish. The problem with this legend is that Coors has never run an ad campaign featuring the slogan *Turn It Loose*.[7] It is possible that another beer company is to blame, and Coors became the victim of a mutating legend. Or it is possible that the story is utterly untrue, a hoax from the beginning.

One case where the legend definitely changed companies is the infamous *Fly Naked* slogan. Allegedly, an airline, either American or Braniff depending on the version, used the slogan *Fly in Leather* to advertise their new leather seats. The slogan was translated into Spanish as *vuela en cuero*, which means, "fly in leather." The problem is that *en cueros* is a colloquialism in some Spanish dialects meaning naked. Hilarity and plummeting sales supposedly ensued. The connection to American Airlines, however, is false; the company never had such a campaign.

Braniff remains a possibility. Around 1987, when the failing airline was on its last legs, it did install leather seating in coach class and featured the new seats in their marketing. Unfortunately, Braniff is no more, and there is no one left to ask whether such a campaign existed and whether it was effective or considered a joke. If there was such an ad campaign, it seems probable that no one ever actually misinterpreted the ad and that ticket sales were never seriously affected. Rather, like Chevy Nova or "Ich bin ein Berliner," the legend probably arose with nitpicking wags who were poking fun at the failing company.

These business mistranslations would simply be funny, harmless stories (even the negative images unfairly bestowed on companies like Coors or American Airlines are minor and probably insignificant) if it were not for the fact that they are often vectored in business school textbooks, newspaper articles, and marketing collateral for translation and international marketing services.

These legends do not just appear in e-mail lists of the "ten greatest marketing mistakes." They are frequently presented at business forums as actual case studies of international marketing problems. They create the perception that international marketing is more hazardous and difficult than it actually is, and serve to dissuade some businesses from marketing products abroad or in making them spend money on expensive consulting services.

Some might say that the actual truth is irrelevant, that caution in translating ads and slogans is justified and necessary. There certainly is potential for error in translation, but most companies and marketing professionals are keenly aware of this and exercise due caution. If they did not do so, we would have many, easily verifiable examples. Inelegant phrasing and spelling errors in translation are more likely than serious embarrassment due to unintended vulgarity. In this respect these legends are much like the classic urban legend of the kidney theft. In it, a businessman visits the big city and engages the services of a prostitute, only to wake up in the morning missing a kidney.

Now there are many good reasons for not consorting with prostitutes, but kidney theft is not one of them. Inventing fictional boogeymen only leads to unnecessary levels of concern and money being spent to solve nonexistent problems.

Translation mistakes are not the only mythical problems encountered by those dealing with other languages. Sometimes the process of translation itself comes under fire. There are numerous legends about how a particular word or phrase actually means, "I do not understand" in a local language or dialect, and how the translator assumes that this reply is the name for something.

Kangaroo

Perhaps the most famous of these "I do not understand" legends is the alleged origin of the word *kangaroo*. The story goes that when white men first saw the strange creature, they eagerly asked the local Aborigines what the animal was called. They asked, of course, in English, and presumably loudly and very slowly. The Aborigines responded by saying, "kangaroo," meaning, "I do not understand." The English took this to be the name of the animal. This fanciful story appears only relatively recently and has no supporting evidence, so it is almost certainly false.

The name for this antipodean quadruped dates, in English at least, to 1770 when Captain Cook recorded it as an Aboriginal name for the animal: "The animals which I have before mentioned, called by the Natives Kangooroo or Kanguru." Cook's shipboard naturalist, Sir Joseph Banks, confirms this: "The largest was called by the natives kangooroo."

The legend probably got its start some decades later when subsequent expeditions discovered that different Aboriginal groups had different names for the animal, and they could not identify one that had a name similar to *kangaroo*. Therefore they thought Cook and Banks were mistaken. Watkin Tench, a marine accompanying the first shipment of convicts to Australia, writes in his 1793 *Complete Account of the Settlement at Port Jackson*: "The large, or grey kanguroo, to which the natives give the name of Pat-ag-a-ran. Note, Kanguroo was a name unknown to them for any animal, until we introduced it."[8]

Other nineteenth-century researchers had similar problems finding a native origin for *kangaroo*. More recent linguistic fieldwork, however, has found the Aboriginal origin. It is from the Guugu Yimidhirr, an Aboriginal language of the Endeavour River region of Queensland, word *gangurru*.[9]

Gringo

Kangaroo shows us that these legends about translation are nothing new. Another word often thought to stem from a mistranslation is *gringo*. This term for white English-speaking Americans has an interesting story attached to its etymology. Unfortunately, like so many of the interesting stories recounted in these pages, this one is not true.

The story goes that the name originated during the 1846–48 Mexican–American War. Supposedly, Yankee soldiers were fond of singing a song, based on a Robert Burns poem that was popular at the time, the refrain of which went "Green grow the rushes, O." (Alternate versions of the tale give it as "Green grow the lilacs.") The Mexicans, probably as tired of hearing the song as you are of the latest Top-40 hit, began calling the Americans "green grows," which eventually became *gringos*.

The story does have some facts to recommend it, notably the timing of its entry into English. The earliest English-language citation of *gringo* in the *OED2* is from 1849 by John Wood-house Audubon, the son of the famous artist. Also, the song in question was indeed popular during the war years. In a variant of the tale it was not the Yankees who were singing the song, but rather Irish volunteers in Bolivar's army. While this would take the origin of the term back a few decades to 1819, it is not far enough back.

While the earliest English-language usage is indeed from the 1840s, the earliest use of *gringo* in Spanish is considerably older than the Mexican–American War or Bolivar's 1819 campaign. The word appears in the *Diccionario Castellano* in 1787, which says that it was used in Malaga to refer to anyone who spoke Spanish badly, and in Madrid in reference to the Irish. *Gringo* probably comes from the Spanish *griego*, or Greek. So it is akin to the phrase *it is Greek to me.*

Given its 1849 English debut, it seems likely that the word was brought into English by U.S. soldiers returning from the Mexican War, but it is a simple borrowing and has nothing to do with any songs.

Conclusion

So where does all this leave us? We've examined various patterns and methods of distribution of linguistic legends. The reasons we tell these linguistic legends are myriad. People affected by racism tend to find racist origins in words. Those who are nautical enthusiasts favor nautical explanations. Those whose native dialects are associated with the lower strata of society will gravitate toward legends like Elizabethan English being spoken in the Appalachians. We tell these stories because

- They are simply good stories.
- They strengthen and validate group identity.
- They reinforce negative, racist, and xenophobic ideas about others.
- They appeal to our interests, such as ships and the sea.

- They serve a political purpose.
- They lampoon the high and mighty.
- They serve an economic purpose, justifying some type of business venture.
- They are attempts to promote euphemism, ascribing socially acceptable origins to unseemly words and phrases.
- They are examples of word play and humor and sometimes deliberate hoaxes.
- They explain mysteries.

But above all, people repeat these legends to bolster their beliefs about society or how they would like society to be.

How should we deal with such stories when we hear them? We should treat them skeptically. Skepticism does not mean that we automatically dismiss such stories when we hear them, but rather we should examine the evidence objectively. We should not accept such stories at face value. The key is examining the evidence and not simply believing something because someone claims it is true. In this way we can separate the bunk from the truth.

The results may be disappointing to some. They may lose an argument that supports their worldview, or they may simply lose a fun story that they like to tell. But the truth does not have to be boring. Skeptics do not have to be spoilsports. There are plenty of good linguistic tales that are not bunk. In fact, the origin of *bunk* is one of them.

The word *bunk* is short for *bunkum*, which in turn is an alteration of *Buncombe*, the name of a county in North Carolina. In 1820, the Missouri Question, whether Missouri should be admitted to the Union as a slave or a free state, was being hotly debated in Congress. Near the end of the debate and amidst calls from the floor to have a vote, Felix Walker, the representative from Buncombe rose to speak. Walker launched into a long and irrelevant speech. When asked by other members to desist, he replied that he was bound to "make a speech for Buncombe," and continued to speak—thus, the word *bunk* was born.[1]

Another such origin is that of the mathematical term *googol*. In 1940, mathematician Edward Kasner asked his nephew, nine-year-old Milton Sirotta, to think up a term for a really big number, 10^{100} or a one followed by one hundred zeroes. Young Sirotta quickly responded with *googol*, and then went one better and said that a googol of googols should be called a *googolplex*.[2]

Or there is the famous case of John Montagu, the fourth Earl of Sandwich (1718–92), a notorious gambler who once refused to leave the gaming table to eat, ordering a servant to bring him two slices of bread with slices of beef in between. Such was the birth of the *sandwich*.[3]

There are many such gems to found, all the more lustrous because they are true. Those of us who stand up and call for skepticism and reason know that there is little chance that we can stop the spread of these legends. And even if we occasionally have a victory and quash a false legend here and there, another will rise up and take its place. Some might say we should sit down and keep our peace. But we don't. In a way we are all making speeches "for Buncombe." It does not really matter how many are listening. We have something to say, and in the off chance that someone is listening, we will say it.

In the end, whether these stories are true or whether they are false is not really the point. What is important is the process we use to evaluate them, that we engage the brains nature gave us and examine the evidence and arguments critically.

Notes /nōts/

Abbreviations

In the following notes, several abbreviations are used for frequently cited works. They are listed below for the reader's convenience.

ADS-L *American Dialect Society Email Discussion List*, available at http://www.americandialect.org/adslarchive.html
AHD4 *American Heritage Dictionary*, 4th edition, Houghton Mifflin, 2000.
DARE *Dictionary of American Regional English*, Frederic C. Cassidy and Joan Houston Hall, eds., Belknap Press, Vol. I: A-C, 1985; Vol. II: D-H, 1991; Vol. III: I-O, 1996; Vol. IV: P-Sk, 2002.
HDAS *Historical Dictionary of American Slang*, J. E. Lighter, ed. Random House, Vol. I: A-G, 1994; Vol. II: H-O, 1997.
OED2 *Oxford English Dictionary*, 2nd edition, Oxford University Press, 1989.
OED3 *Oxford English Dictionary Online*, new edition, May 2003. Used to reference new material in the online edition that does not appear in the 2nd print edition. Available at http://www.oed.com

Introduction

1. *OED3*, *urban*, a. and n.

2. Peter Van der Linden and Terry Chan, "Alt.folklore.urban frequently asked questions list" available at http://tafkac.org (last accessed 21 July 2004).
3. Shelby Foote, *The Civil War: A Narrative, Fredericksburg to Meridian*, Vintage Books, 1986, pp. 233–34.

Chapter 1: Debunking the Big Boys

1. Iona and Peter Opie, *The Oxford Dictionary of Nursery Rhymes*, new edition, Oxford University Press, 1997, pp. 433–35. This source gives a comprehensive summary of the development of the *Ring around the Rosie* rhyme and a discussion of the variants.
2. William Wells Newell, *Games and Songs of American Children*, 2nd edition, 1903, Dover Reprint, 1963, pp. 127–28.
3. *OED2, rose*, n.[1] and a.[1], sense #10.
4. Allen Walker Read's seminal *American Speech* articles on the etymology of 'OK' are "The First Stage in the History of 'O.K.'," Vol. 38, No. 1, Feb. 1963, pp. 5–27; "The Second Stage in the History of 'O.K.'," Vol. 38, No. 2, May 1963, pp. 83–102; "The Folklore of 'O.K.'," Vol. 39, No. 1, Feb. 1964, pp. 5–25; "Later Stages in the History of 'O.K.'," Vol. 39, No. 2, May 1964, pp. 83–101; "Successive Revisions in the Explanation of 'O.K.'," Vol. 39, No. 4, Dec. 1964, pp. 243–67.
5. Allen Walker Read, "Could Andrew Jackson Spell?" *American Speech*, Vol. 38, No. 3, Oct. 1963, pp. 188–95.
6. Woodford A. Heflin, " 'O.K.', But What Do We Know about It?" *American Speech*, Vol. 16, No. 2, Apr. 1941, pp. 89, 92. This article contains reproductions of the three questionable documents.
7. Heflin, pp. 89–91.

8. Heflin, pp. 88, 93–95; Albert Matthews, "A Note on 'O.K.'," *American Speech*, Vol. 16, No. 4, Dec. 1941, pp. 257–59. Heflin argues in favor of the 1815 document being an early use of 'OK'; Matthews conclusively debunks this argument.

9. *HDAS, nine*, n.

10. *HDAS, nine*, n.

11. "The State of Ready-Mix Trucks in 1964," *Ready Mixed Concrete*, Aug. 1964, p. 1014.

12. Carole Sheffield, "Sexual Terrorism," in Jo Freeman, ed., *Women: A Feminist Perspective*, Mayfield Publishing, 1989, p. 7.

13. Sir William Blackstone, *Commentaries on the Laws of England*, 176569, Book 1, Chap. XV.

14. Elizabeth Pleck, "Wife Beating in Nineteenth-Century America," in *Victimology: An International Journal*, Vol. 4, 1979, p. 61.

15. Pleck, p. 71.

16. *Bradley v. The State*, Walker 156, Miss. 1824

17. *State v. A.B. Rhodes* (61 N.C. 453), 1868.

18. *State v. Oliver* (70 N.C. 61), 1874.

19. Del Martin, *Battered Wives*, Volcano Press, 1976, p. 31.

20. Terry Davidson, "Wife Beating: A Recurring Phenomenon Throughout History," in Maria Roy, ed., *Battered Women*, Van Nostrand Reinhold, 1977, p. 18.

21. U.S. Commission on Civil Rights, *Under the Rule of Thumb: Battered Women and the Administration of Justice*, Jan. 1982, p. 2.

22. *OED2, rule of thumb.*

23. Douglas Martin, "Ray Hicks, Who Told Yarns Older Than America, Dies at 80," *New York Times*, 27 Apr. 2003, sec. 1, p. 47.

24. Zell Miller, *The Mountains Within Me*, Cherokee Publishing, 1985, pp. 79, 81.

25. North Carolina Department of Commerce, Travel and Tourism Division, *A Dictionary of the Queen's English*, n.p., ca. 1965.
26. Metcalf, Allan, *How We Talk: American Regional English Today*, Houghton Mifflin, 2000, pp. 62–63.
27. *DARE*, Vol. I, 1985, *afear(e)d*, adj.
28. *DARE*, Vol. III, *learn*, v. B.1.
29. *OED2*, *learn*, v.
30. *DARE*, Vol. II, *help* v.
31. *OED2*, *hap*, v.[2] and n.[2]; *DARE*, Vol. II, *hap*, n.
32. *OED2*, *neb*, n. and v.; *DARE*, Vol. III, *neb*, n. and v.
33. *OED2*, *flake*, n.[1]; *DARE*, Vol. II, *flake*, n.[1]
34. Another excellent debunking of this myth can be found in Michael Montgomery's "In the Appalachians They Speak Like Shakespeare," in *Language Myths*, Laurie Bauer and Peter Trudgill, eds., Penguin, 1998.
35. I am hardly the first to debunk this myth. Laura Martin was the first in "Eskimo Words For Snow," *American Anthropologist*, Vol. 88, No. 2, June 1986. Geoffrey Pullam published a more popular debunking in *The Great Eskimo Vocabulary Hoax*, University of Chicago Press, 1991. Stephen Pinker summarized the debunking in this best-selling book *The Language Instinct*, William Morrow, 1994. Still, the myth persists.
36. Franz Boas, *The Handbook of North American Indians*, Vol. I, Smithsonian Institution, 1911.
37. Benjamin Lee Whorf, "Science and Linguistics," available at http://www.lcc.gatech.edu/~herrington/classes/6320f01/whorf.html (last accessed 21 July 2004), originally published in *Technology Review* Vol. 42, No. 6, Massachusetts Institute of Technology, April 1940.
38. Michael Fortescue, *West Greenlandic*, Croom Helm, 1984.

39. "Weather Word," Chicago Tribune, 23 Aug. 2001, sec. 2, p. 10, col. 1; Rick Kogan, "Any Way The Wind Blows," *Chicago Tribune*, 2 May 1999; and David Traxel, "The Devil In The White City," *New York Times*, 9 Mar. 2003, sec.7, p. 15, col. 1. And lest we blame newspapers to the exclusion of others, note that the Chicago Historical Society's website gets the origin wrong as well, see http://www.chicagohs.org/history/expo.html (last accessed 16 May 2003).

40. Mitford Mathews, *A Dictionary of Americanisms*, University of Chicago Press, 1951, *windy city*; OED2, *windy*, a.9.

41. Barry Popik, "Windy City" (12 February 1877); "Jazz notes," *ADS-L*, 6 Aug. 2003.

42. Barry Popik, "Fakir" (1875); "Municipality of Wind" (1875); *ADS-L*, 25 Sep. 2003; Barry Popik, "Brooklyn Eagle etymologics," *ADS-L*, 27 Feb. 2003; Barry Popik, "Windy City" (13 November 1879)," *ADS-L*, 26 June 2003, *Cincinnati Enquirer*, p. 1, col. 1, "GRANT. His Big Boom at Chicago. A Warm and Wet Welcome to the Windy City"; Barry Popik, "Windy City (17 July 1880)," *ADS-L*, 19 June 2003: 17 July 1880, "Off For Chicago," *Cincinnati Enquirer*, p. 4, col. 5, "Both nags were in apple-pie condition, and will give a good account of themselves in the Windy City"; Barry Popik, "Cincinnatta (1882); Windy City (September 11, 1882)," *ADS-L*, 29 Apr. 2003: 11 Sep. 1882, *Cincinnati Enquirer*, p. 1, col. 2: "CHICAGO'S RECORD. Crimes of a Day In the Windy City"; Barry Popik, "Windy City (1883)," *ADS-L*, 4 Nov. 2002: 20 Oct., National Police Gazette, pg. 11, "It was here that the late lamented Hulbert, president of the Chicagos, saw him and signed him for the Windy City club. . ."; Barry Popik, "Windy City (1885)," *ADS-L*, 12 Feb. 2000: 19 Sep. 1885, *Cleveland Gazette*, "From the Windy City: Judge Foote's Civil Right decision."

43. Barry Popik, "*NY Sun* Editor Charles Dana neither Originated nor Popularized Chicago's Nickname 'The Windy City,'" *Comments on Etymology*, Vol. 31. No. 3, Dec. 2001, p. 7.
44. *HDAS*, *hot dog*, n. 2.a.
45. *HDAS*, *dog*, n. 7.
46. J. S. Farmer and W. E. Henley, *Slang and Its Analogues*, Vol. II, n.p., 1891, p. 303.
47. Gerald Cohen, "'Hot dog' cartoon," *ADS-L*, 25 June 1999. It would be remiss not to mention that much of the research on the origin of *hot dog* is the work of Barry Popik and first published with Cohen in *Comments on Etymology* in 1995.

Chapter 2: The Elizabethan E-mail Hoax

1. Anon, "Life in the 1500's-Bullshit or Nonsense?" Usenet: alt.folklore.urban, 8 Apr. 1999.
2. Wolfgang Mieder, "(Don't) Throw The Baby Out With The Bathwater," DeProverbio.com, *The Electronic Journal of International Proverb Studies*, Vol. I, No. 1, 1995, available at http:// www.utas.edu.au/docs/flonta/DP,1,1,95/BABY.html (last accessed 21 July 2004).
3. *OED2*, *cat and dog*.
4. *OED2*, *dirt*, n.
5. *OED2*, *threshold*, n., *thresh*, v., and *thrash*, *thresh*, n.[2]
6. *OED2*, *pease*, n.; Opie, *Oxford Dictionary of Nursery Rhymes*, pp. 406–8.
7. *HDAS*, *bacon*, n.
8. *OED2*, *chew*, v. 3.d.; *HDAS*, *chew* , v. 4.
9. *OED2*, *trencher*.[1]
10. *OED2*, *trench*, n. 10.

11. *OED2*, *board*, n. 7a.
12. *OED2*, *upper*, a. 13.
13. *OED2*, *wake*, n.^{1}.
14. *HDAS*, *graveyard shift*; *graveyard watch*.
15. *OED2*, *saved*, ppl.a.
16. *OED2*, *ring*, v.^{2} 11.b.; *ringer*^{2} 3.

Chapter 3: Posh, Phat Pommies

1. H. L. Mencken, *The American Language, Supplement I*, Knopf, 1945, p. 287.
2. Barbara Flora, "Fabulous bit of historiacl [*sic*] knowledge," Usenet: umn.ee.chatter, 7 Aug. 2002.
3. Anon., "origin of shit," Usenet: rec.humor, 12 Apr. 1999.
4. Anon., "Re: (S.H.I.T)," Usenet: rec.aviation.rotorcraft, 30 Jan. 1999.
5. *OED2*, *shit*, *shite*, v. and *shit*, int.
6. *OED2*, *Colinderies* and Richard W. Bailey, *Nineteenth Century English*, University of Michigan Press, 1996, p. 154.
7. U.S. Patent and Trademark Office, Trademark Electronic Search System (TESS), Registration # 0037299, available at http://www. uspto.gov/main/trademarks.htm (last accessed 21 July 2004).
8. Classified ad, *Washington Post*, 26 Dec. 1902, p. 5.
9. *OED2*, *Anzac*.
10. *OED2*, *acronym*.
11. Arndt and Gingrich Bauer, *Greek-English Lexicon of the New Testament*, University of Chicago Press, 1957, p. 385; Ramond E. Brown, *Anchor Bible Commentary on the Gospel of John*, Vol. 1, Doubleday, 1966, p. 246.
12. *OED2*, *cabal*, n.^{1} and *cabala*.

13. *OED2*, radar, scuba.
14. David K. Barnhart, and Allan A. Metcalf, *America In So Many Words*, Houghton Mifflin, 1997, p. 160; e-mail correspondence between the author and Metcalf, 17 Mar. 2003.
15. H. L. Mencken, *The American Language, Supplement I*, Knopf, 1945, p. 410n3. The quote is from Bell Irvin Wiley, *The Plain People of the Confederacy*, n.p., 1944, p. 31.
16. Benjamin Franklin Butler, "Letter to John Albion Andrew," 25 Oct. 1861, in *Private and Official Correspondence of Gen. Benjamin F. Butler, During the Period of the Civil War*, Vol. 1, Marshall, Jessie Ames, ed., Plimpton Press, 1917, p. 669. Thanks to Barry Popik who has uncovered forty different uses of "absent without leave" from various Civil War–era documents. He found no uses of the abbreviation *A.W.O.L.*, however.
17. *AWOL-All Wrong Old Laddiebuck* (film), American Motion Picture Co., ca. 1919. Found in Library of Congress's American Memory Database, available at http://www.loc.gov
18. Jesse Sheidlower, *The F Word*, 2nd edition, Random House, 1999, pp. 117–18.
19. Carl Darling Buck, *A Dictionary of Selected Synonyms in the Principal Indo–European Languages*, University of Chicago Press, 1949, p. 279.
20. John Ayto, *Dictionary of Word Origins*, Arcade Publishing, 1990.
21. Allan Walker Read, "Where Does That Word Come From?" *Milestones in the History of English in America*, Richard W. Bailey, ed., Publication of the American Dialect Society (PADS 86), Duke University Press, 2002. This "essay" is actually a series of 1971 letters between Read and other linguists on the validity of Buck's citation from 1278. No one could provide evidence of where the citation came from and the consensus was that if genuine, it was not an instance of *fuck*.

22. Sheidlower, pp. xxxiii, xi. In other versions of this tale it is Tallulah Bankhead who makes the quip, not Parker. This alleged quote may be an urban legend in itself.

23. Rich Payne, "Re: Giving the bird . . . ," Usenet: rec.org. mensa, 19 Dec. 1996.

24. Tom and Ray Magliozzi, *Car Talk*, Show # 9613, National Public Radio, 28 Mar. 1996.

25. *OED2*, *news*, n. (pl.).

26. *OED2*, *tip*, v.[4]

27. *OED2*, *golf*, n.

28. J. R. R. Tolkien, *The Hobbit*, revised edition, Ballantine, 1966, p. 30.

29. Mario Pei, *The Story of Language*, J. B. Lippincott, 1949, p. 214. Thanks to Carol Braham for finding this 1949 citation for me.

30. *OED2*, *spud*, n.

31. Mario Pei, *The Story of Language*, revised edition, J. B. Lippincott, 1965, p. 223.

32. Adrian Room, *Trade Name Origins*, NTC Publishing Group, 1982, pp. 128–29.

33. *Du Pont Context*, Vol. 7, No. 2, 1978.

34. *OED2*, *nylon*.

35. *OED2*, *S.O.S.*, n.

36. *OED2*, *Pommy*, n. (a.), *Pom*[2].

37. *OED2*, *fat*, a and n.[2]; *OED3*, *phat*, a.

38. *OED2*, *posh*, a., *posh*, n.[2]

39. *Merriam-Webster New Book of Word Histories*, Merriam-Webster, 1991, pp. 372–74.

Chapter 4: Canoe

1. *OED2*, *devil*, n. 22.j.

2. *OED2*, *devil*, n. 13. and *pay*, v.[2].
3. *OED2*, *cat-o'-nine-tails*, n.
4. *OED2*, *bag*, n. 19.
5. *OED2*, *swing*, v[1].
6. C. Nepean Longridge, *The Anatomy of Nelson's Ships*, Naval Institute Press, 1981, p. 64.
7. Herman Melville, *Omoo*, Chapter LIII, "Farming in Polynesia," 1847, text available at http://ibiblio.org/gutenberg/etext03/omoo10. txt (last accessed 21 July 2004).
8. *HDAS*, *brass monkey*.
9. *OED3*, *monkey tail*, n.
10. *OED2*, *barrel*, n.
11. *OED2*, *queue*, n.
12. *OED2*, *P*, 3.
13. "Editor's Drawer," *Harper's New Monthly Magazine*, Vol. 4, No. 20, Jan. 1852, p. 270.
14. *OED2*, *weather*, n., 2.f.
15. *OED2*, *knock*, v., 12.
16. *OED2*, *gun*, n., 6.c.
17. *HDAS*, *ball*, v.
18. *HDAS*, *balls to the wall*.
19. Nia Vardalos, *My Big Fat Greek Wedding* (film), IFC Films, 2002.
20. *OED2*, *lynch law, lynch*, v.
21. Robert McCrum, et al., *The Story of English*, 3rd revised edition, Penguin, 2002, p. 236.
22. *HDAS*, *jasm*, n.
23. *HDAS*, *jism*, n.
24. Geoffrey Ward and Ken Burns, *Jazz: A History of America's Music*, Knopf, 2000, p. 65.
25. *HDAS*, *jazz*, n. & v.
26. *HDAS*, *jazz*, v.
27. *OED2*, *jazz*, n.

28. *HDAS, jazz*, n. 3.

29. Gerald Cohen, "Jazz Revisited," *Comments on Etymology*, Vol. 32, Nos. 4–5, Dec. 2002–Jan. 2003, pp. 9–11.

30. H. L. Mencken, *The American Language, Supplement II*, Knopf, 1948, p. 709.

31. Cohen, "Jazz Revisited," pp. 15–16.

32. E. T. Gleeson, "I Remember the Birth of Jazz," *The Call-Bulletin*, 3 Sep. 1938, p. 3, col. 1, reprinted in Cohen, "Jazz Revisited."

33. Cohen, "Jazz Revisited," p. 44.

34. Cohen, "Jazz Revisited," pp. 33–34.

35. *HDAS, jazz*, n.

36. George Thompson, "'Jazz' in the LA Times, 1912 & 1917," *ADS-L*, 4 Aug. 2003, and Barry Popik, "Windy City (12 February 1877); Jazz notes," *ADS-L*, 6 Aug. 2003; the original citation is *Los Angeles Times*, 2 Apr. 1912, part III, pg. 2, col. 1.

37. Allan Walker Read, "The Claims For a Native Source of the Name *America*," 1985, in *America-Naming the Country and Its People*, Studies in Onomastics, Vol. 4, Edwin Mellen Press, 2001, pp. 2–3.

38. Jules Marcou, Jules, "Origin of the Name America," *The Atlantic Monthly*, March 1875, p. 293.

39. Marcou, p. 292.

40. Read, "Claims For a Native Source . . . ," pp. 3–8.

41. Rodney Broome, *Terra Incognita*, Educare Press, 2001, pp. 111–12.

Chapter 5: Harlots, Hookers, and Condoms

1. Shelby Foote, *The Civil War: A Narrative, Fredericksburg to Meridian*, Vintage Books, 1986, pp. 233–34.

2. *OED2, hooker¹.*
3. *HDAS, hooker³.*
4. *OED2, hooker².*
5. *OED2, harlot,* n.
6. William E. Kruck, *Looking For Dr. Condom,* Publication of the American Dialect Society #66, University of Alabama Press, 1981, pp. 1–2.
7. Kruck, p. 26.
8. Kruck, p. 52.
9. Kruck, p. 26.
10. Ronald L. George, "The History of Plumbing, Part 2 — Renaissance Conveniences Yield to Modern Sanitation," *Plumbing Engineer,* Apr. 2001, p. 45.
11. *OED2, crap,* n.¹
12. *OED2, dunny,* n.²
13. *OED2, crab,* n.¹ and *craps.*
14. Edwin H. Miller, "More Air Force Slang," *American Speech,* Vol. 21, No. 4., Dec. 1946, p. 310.
15. Barry Popik, "In like Flynn; Run for the Roses; Yoot," *ADS-L,* 12 June 1999.
16. *San Francisco Examiner,* 8 Feb. 1942, Sports Section, pg. 2, col. 1.
17. *San Francisco Call-Bulletin,* 9 Feb. 1943, pg. 7, col. 5.
18. The facts of McCoy's life that are recounted here are taken from Robert Cantwell, *The Real McCoy,* Auerbach, 1971.
19. *HDAS,* McCoy, n.
20. Fred Shapiro, "More Evidence on 'The Real McCoy,' " *ADS-L,* 20 July 2003, citation from *Los Angeles Times,* 19 Sep. 1904, p. 6
21. *HDAS,* McCoy, n.
22. Barry Popik, "Real McCoy (1914, 1915, 1916)," *ADS-L,* 8 July 2003, citation from *Nevada State Journal,* 14 Dec. 1914, pg. 6, col. 1.

23. *Boy's Own Paper*, 4 May 1901, cited in Jonathan Green, "Re: Real McCoy (1914, 1915, 1916)," *ADS-L*, 9 July 2003.
24. *HDAS, Dixie*, n.
25. Mitford M. Mathews, "Of Matters Lexicographical," *American Speech*, Vol. 26, No. 4., Dec. 1951, pp. 288.
26. *HDAS, Dixie*, n.
27. Newell, pp. 221–222.
28. George Thompson, "'Upset' in horseracing," *ADS-L*, 12 Nov. 2002.
29. OED2, *pumpernickel*; and Barry Popik, "Pumpernickel (1756); Mish-Mash, Antipasto (1617)," *ADS-L*, 1 May 2002.
30. Francis Ford Coppola and Mario Puzo, *The Godfather, Part II* (film), Paramount Pictures, 1974.
31. Marion L. Smith, "American Names/Declaring Independence," U.S. Immigration & Naturalization Service, 28 Feb. 2003, available at http://uscis.gov/graphics/aboutus/history/articles/nameessay. html (last accessed 21 July 2004).

Chapter 6: The Perils of Political Correctness

1. *OED2, niggard*, n. and a.; *niger* and *nigger*, n.
2. *OED2, spade*, n.[1] 2.a.
3. *OED2*, spade, n.[2]
4. Edward Sheng-Yang Wang, "Fascinating origins of American English ("fifth column" et al.)," Usenet: soc.culture.asian.american, 11 Dec. 1993.
5. Brian McLean, "A friend sent this to me." Usenet: bit.listserv. blues-l, 26 Sep. 1998.
6. *OED2, picnic*, n.
7. "Minister Attacked Over 'Racist' Term," *BBC News*, 15 May 2002, available at http://news.bbc.co.uk/1/hi/uk_politics/1988681.stm (last accessed 21 July 2004).

8. *HDAS, nitty gritty*, n.
9. *DARE, jimmies*, n.pl.[2]
10. Ted Frank, "Re: Nitrous oxide abuse and sprinkles in Carmel," Usenet: alt.folklore.urban, 28 Oct. 1997.
11. Seth Deitch, "Re: Nitrous oxide abuse and sprinkles in Carmel," Usenet: alt.folklore.urban, 31 Oct. 1997. Deitch is quoting another poster here, not making this contention himself. The original post making the Jim Crow connection does not appear in the Google archives.
12. Mathews, Dict. Of Amer., *Jim Crow car*.
13. *HDAS, jimmy*, n.
14. Matthew Alice, "Straight From the Hip," *San Diego Reader*, Jan. 1998; Jan Freeman, "Gimme Jimmies!" *Boston Globe*, 9 Feb. 2003, p. D3; and e-mail correspondence between the author and the Just Born company, 27 May 2003.
15. George Carlin, *Brain Droppings*, Hyperion Press, 1997, p. 165.
16. *OED2, India*.
17. *OED2, Hindustani, Hindoostani*, a. and n.; *Hindu, Hindoo*, n. and a.
18. Peter Matthiessen, *Indian Country*, Penguin, 1992, p. 2.
19. Letter, Christopher Columbus to Raphael Sanxis, "Concerning the Islands Recently Discovered in the Indian Sea," 1493, available at http://www.usm.maine.edu/~maps/columbus/toc.html (last accessed 21 July 2004).
20. *OED2, Indian*, a. and n., 4.b.
21. *OED2, squaw*, n. (and a.).
22. Douglas Leechman, and Robert A. Hall, Jr., "American Indian Pidgin English: Attestations and Grammatical Peculiarities," *American Speech*, Vol. 30, No. 3., Oct. 1955, p. 169.
23. Leechman, p. 166–67.
24. E. Cobham Brewer, *Dictionary of Phrase and Fable*, 1898, available at http://www.bartleby.com/81/ (last accessed 21 July 2004).
25. *OED2, hip*, int. (n.[4])

26. *OED2*, *hurrah, hurray*, int. and n.
27. *HDAS*, *gay*, adj.
28. Dudley Nichols and Hagar Wilde, *Bringing Up Baby* (film), RKO Radio Pictures, 1938.
29. *HDAS*, *gaycat*, n.
30. *HDAS*, *gay*, adj.
31. *OED2*, *faggot*, n.
32. *OED2*, *fag* v¹ and n¹.
33. *OED2*, *fag* n⁴ and n².
34. *OED2*, *handicap*, n. and *handicap*, v.
35. David Mayer, David, "Commentary: Postmodernism and the Jefferson-Hemings Myth," Apr. 2001, available at http://www.objectivistcenter.org/articles/dmayer_postmodernism -jeffersonhemings-myth.asp (last accessed 21 July 2004).
36. *OED3*, *politically*, adv. 3.b.
37. *OED2*, *P*, II.a.
38. William Safire, *Safire's New Political Dictionary*, Random House, 1993, *politically correct*.
39. Mao Zedong, "Where Do Correct Ideas Come From?," *Four Essays on Philosophy*, Foreign Languages Press, 1968.
40. *OED2*, *tinker*, n. and *tinkler*¹.
41. *OED2*, *tink*, v¹.

Chapter 7: Wax Tadpoles and Jelly Doughnuts

1. Bernard Gwertzman, "Interpreter's Gaffes Embarrass State Dept.," *New York Times*, 31 Dec. 1977, pp. A1–A2.
2. John F. Kennedy, Speech: "Remarks in the Rudolph Wilde Platz," 26 June 1963, available at http://www.cs.umb.edu/ jfklibrary/ jo62663.htm (last accessed 21 July 2004).
3. Jürgen Eichoff, "Ich bin ein Berliner: A History and a Linguistic Clarification," *Monatshefte*, Vol. 85, No. 1, Spring 1993, p. 71.

4. David A. Ricks, *Blunders in International Business,* Blackwell Publishers, 1993, p. 35.
5. Frances R. Hammond, "Letter to David Mikkelson," 5 Aug. 1993, available on Usenet: alt.folklore.urban, "Re: Chevrolet Nova," 28 Sep. 1993.
6. H. F. Allman, "Transliteration of Coca-Cola Trademark to Chinese Characters," *Coca-Cola Overseas,* June 1957. Citation provided by David Mikkelson; the full article is available at http://tafkac.org/products/coca-cola/coca-cola_chinese.html (last accessed 21 July 2004).
7. Coors Brewing Company, letter to the author, 19 June 2003.
8. *OED2, kangaroo,* n.
9. *AHD4, kangaroo.*

Conclusion

1. *OED2, buncombe, bunkum.*
2. *OED2, googol.*
3. *OED2, sandwich* n².

Selected Annotated
Bibliography /ˌbiblēˈägrəfē/

Alt.Folklore.Urban Archive, http://tafkac.org, 2003. A compilation of postings to the Usenet group alt.folklore.urban, arranged by subject. This site contains a wealth of information on urban legends.

Bauer, Laurie, and Peter Trudgill, editors. *Language Myths*. Penguin, 1998. A collection of essays on misperceptions about language and linguistics.

Brunvand, Jan Harold. *The Vanishing Hitchhiker*. W. W. Norton, 1981. Brunvand is the dean of urban folklorists. He has published a series of popular books detailing traditional urban legends. The books do not address linguistic legends, but are well-researched and highly readable books about modern folklore and its transmission. Other books in the series include *The Choking Doberman* (1984); *The Mexican Pet* (1986); *Curses! Broiled Again!* (1989); and *The Baby Train* (1993).

Cassidy, Frederic G., and Joan Houston Hall, chief editors. *Dictionary of American Regional English*, Vols. I through IV. Belknap Press of Harvard University Press, 1985–2002. An invaluable source for the meaning, history, and usage of regional American words and phrases. Unfortunately, it is not yet complete; only the first four volumes, covering letters A–Sk, have been published.

Lighter, J. E., editor. *Random House Historical Dictionary of American Slang*, Vols. I and II. Random House, 1994 and 1997. An invaluable source for the meaning, history, and usage of nonstandard American words and phrases. Like DARE, it is not complete. Only the first two volumes have been published, covering letters A-O.

Merriam-Webster New Book of Word Histories. Merriam-Webster, 1991. An in-depth discussion of the origin of some 1,500 words.

Mikkelson, David, and Barbara Mikkelson. *Urban Legends Reference Pages,* http:// www.snopes.com, 2003. One of the best sites on the internet for debunking urban legends.

Opie, Iona, and Peter Opie. *Oxford Dictionary of Nursery Rhymes,* New Edition. Oxford University Press, 1997. An excellent single-volume source that traces the development of 449 children's rhymes through the centuries.

Oxford English Dictionary Online, http://www.oed.com. Oxford University Press, 2003. The single best source for information on the meaning, history, and usage of words in the English language.

Pullum, Geoffrey K. *The Great Eskimo Vocabulary Hoax and Other Irreverent Essays on the Study of Language.* University of Chicago Press, 1991. A collection of essays on linguistics, but only the title essay addresses a topic related to linguistic folklore. That essay is, however, an excellent discussion of the Eskimo-snow legend.

Read, Allen Walker. *Milestones in the History of English in America,* ed. Richard W. Bailey. Publication of the American Dialect Society #86, Duke University Press, 2002. This volume compiles many of Read's journal articles published over the course of his long career, and includes the *American Speech* articles in which he traces the history of *OK.*

Index /ˈinˌdeks/

CPSIA information can be obtained
at www.ICGtesting.com
Printed in the USA
BVOW08s0119100517

483668BV00001B/5/P